Miriam's Mantle

LeaderShift:
Changing to Lead, Leading to Change

Janine A. Dailey

Copyright © 2021 Janine A. Dailey

Unless otherwise indicated, all Scripture quotations are taken from the Holy Bible, New Living Translation, copyright © 1996, 2004, 2015 by Tyndale House Foundation. Used by permission of Tyndale House Publishers, Inc., Carol Stream, Illinois 60188. All rights reserved. "Scripture quotations are from the ESV® Bible (The Holy Bible, English Standard Version®), copyright © 2001 by Crossway, a publishing ministry of Good News Publishers. Used by permission. All rights reserved." Scripture quotations from The Authorized (King James) Version. Rights in the Authorized Version in the United Kingdom are vested in the Crown. Reproduced by permission of the Crown's patentee, Cambridge University Press

All rights reserved. No part of this document may be reproduced or transmitted in any form or by any means, electronic, mechanical, photocopying, recording, or otherwise, without prior written permission of the author.

MIRIAM'S MANTLE
LeaderSHIFT: Changing to Lead, Leading to Change

Janine A. Dailey
jdailey@me.com

ISBN 978-1-949826-38-8

Printed in the USA
All rights reserved

Published by: EAGLES GLOBAL BOOKS | Frisco, Texas
In conjunction with the 2021 Eagles Authors Course
Cover & interior designed by DestinedToPublish.com

In loving memory of Patricia Dance, who planted a seed that continues to blossom.

To my mother, who never gave up on me and is still my biggest fan.

To Deborah Fair, my sister, who has seen the power of the dance ministry in our lives. To Jeff Fair, her husband, our recorder of everything.

To my husband, Rev. Rodney Dailey, who understands the power of transformation because we have lived it.

To my children, Amara, Rodney II and Janaya, what a journey, and look at you now!

To every dance ministry leader who loves what they do. Thank you all!

Acknowledgments

Thank you, God, for being the first choreographer of my life. What a dance you created within me.

Thank you, Holy Spirit, for being with me and for allowing me to continue to do the work God began with His first dance.

Table of Contents

Introduction vii

Chapter 1: Miriam's Mantle 1

Chapter 2: Principles of Kingdom Leadership 9

Chapter 3: Your Role as His Kingdom Leader – Taking Care of Yourself. 17

Chapter 4: What's Going On? 27

Chapter 5: Choreography with Purpose. I Want to SEE God! 37

Chapter 6: Developing and Maintaining a Spiritually and Emotionally Healthy Dance Ministry. 47

Chapter 7: Be Fruitful and Multiply. 67

Chapter 8: Ready, Set, Go! 75

Conclusion 81

Endnotes 85

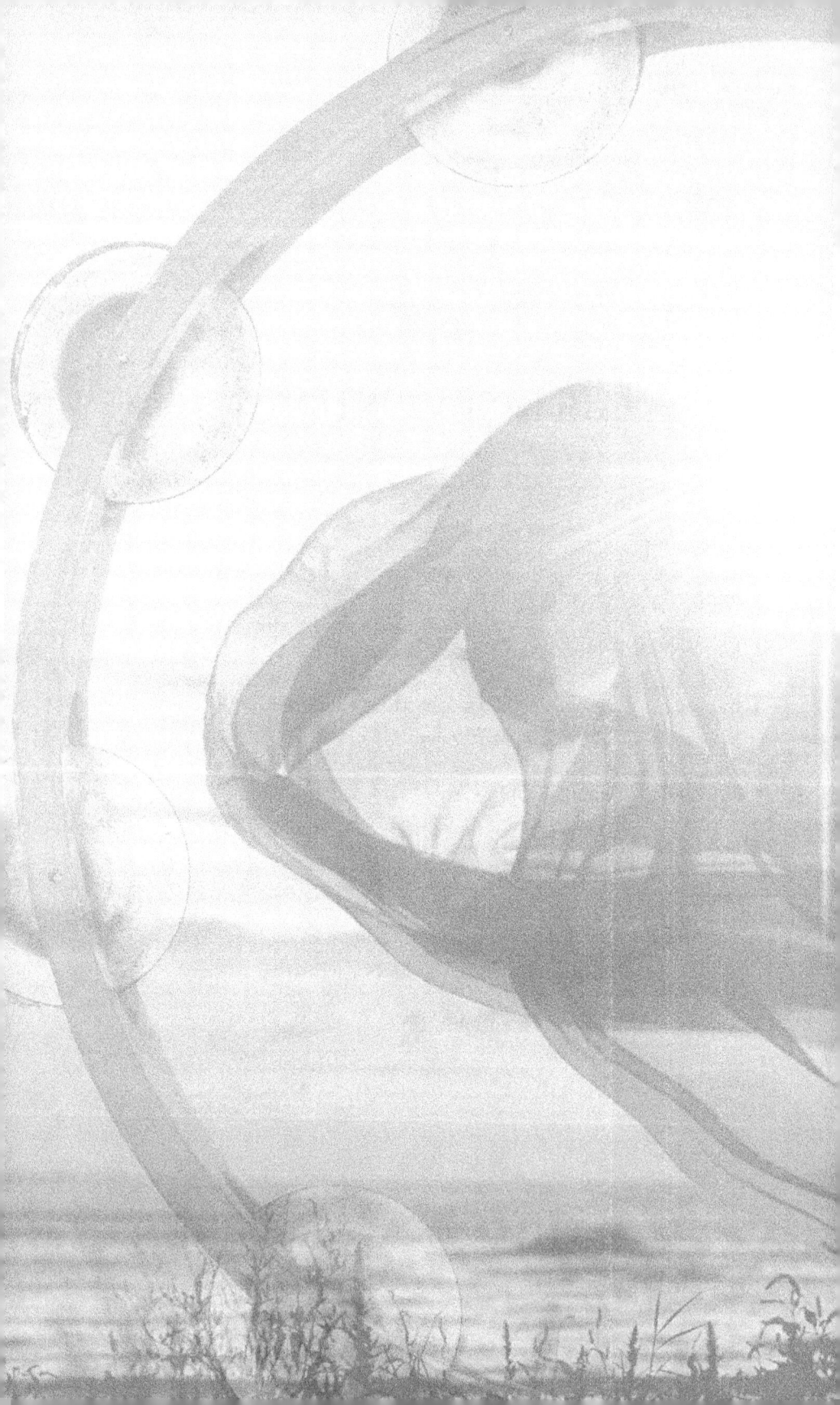

INTRODUCTION

I love to dance. I really love to dance. Did I say I love to dance? My mother signed me up to dance, and by the age of six, I was doing tap, jazz and ballet. In addition to dance, I also ran track and played tennis, but dance would be the only activity I would return to years later.

As a teen, I got lost in the wilderness and had a very difficult time. My self-esteem was low, and I started using drugs and had a few close encounters with death. All throughout the wilderness, I danced – and yes, it was in the club. I could get on the dance floor and dance all night long with whoever wanted to dance, club after club after club. Even then, at the age of 18, although I was not dancing for God, as strange as it may seem, I was thankful to God for dance.

I thank God I made it out of the wilderness. I almost lost my life dancing with too many of the wrong folk, BUT God had a different plan for my life which would include dancing, but now with a different spirit, a different sound and for a different reason.

I discovered the dance ministry at my church one Resurrection Sunday. St. Paul African Methodist Episcopal Church in Cambridge, MA, is the same church where I grew up. I was in awe when I saw the dance ministry. I had never seen dance in church before. I was so moved by what I saw, and it was an experience I remember to this day.

I connected with God that day in a way I had not experienced before in my journey as a believer. I saw God in a new way, I experienced God in a new way and He, God, got my attention in a new way that very day.

A few months later, I joined the dance ministry at my church, and wow, my life has never been the same. It changed my life. I had the urge, the draw to learn more about the ministry, to be the best I could be and, most importantly, to work on my relationship with God. Yes God! It was the first time during my Christian journey that I actually felt compelled to learn more about God. I had a desire to work on my relationship and a burning desire to grow in this ministry of dance. I wanted to know as much as I needed to know in order for me to be the best that I could be.

I had no idea at the time that God was preparing me for greater things. My desire led me to realize that not only did God have a plan for my life, but part of that plan was in the ministry of dance – the very thing that I love, but now I was dancing for God, because of His love, grace and mercy. I was dancing because I was free, I had been delivered. I was dancing because my light was now shining. I was dancing because I could help save others. I was dancing to a different sound, for a different reason and with a new spirit. I was on fire, and God had this planned out for me all along, to do what I love to do – DANCE! And now, I was dancing for the KING. What an amazing privilege.

Dancing for God was one of the ways that I was able to give everything I had and go beyond to give Him my all. It was the purest of myself and the area in which I sacrificed my all to honor God. It was through this ministry that I realized that God saved me from dancing in the streets to using my gift to dance for Him and before Him and His people. WOW! Dancing for God has taken me to different nations, dancing, preaching and teaching. Who could have known? God. Now, I must say, dancing was the entry point for a full life of ministry. God got my attention through dance, and as a result, I have had the awesome privilege to shift nations, regions, cities and churches. Yes, through the ministry of dance. Look at God!

God has given you this amazing opportunity to lead others to a place of worship that will shift and change lives. Although we use dance, it's never about the dance – it's about the anointing, the power and His Spirit that He is releasing upon you so the people can see and experience God visually.

What God has given to you to release in that moment can change every aspect of the worship experience for all those involved. It can break yokes, help set the captives free. It can provide hope in despair, joy in sadness, light in darkness. Yes, through the ministry of dance, God's people can not only hear Him but see Him. Isn't that an amazing thing? God is using you so people can see Him through you.

God has called you for such a time as this to use this amazing visual ministry to preach the gospel, heal the broken-hearted and set the captives free. Your assignment as the leader of the dance ministry is to take that ministry from the known to the unknown – to train them, equip them and empower them so they understand they are not just dancers, but messengers of God with the gift of movement to share His word.

That is what this book is about: the power of dance and the mantle you have been given. As a dance ministry leader, it is important to understand the power, purpose and impact of the ministry God has called you to lead. Your transformation will help others transform. You are *"Changing to lead, leading to change."*

I pray that your eyes and ears will be opened to all the new things God has in store for you as you read through this book. Your NEXT is on the way.

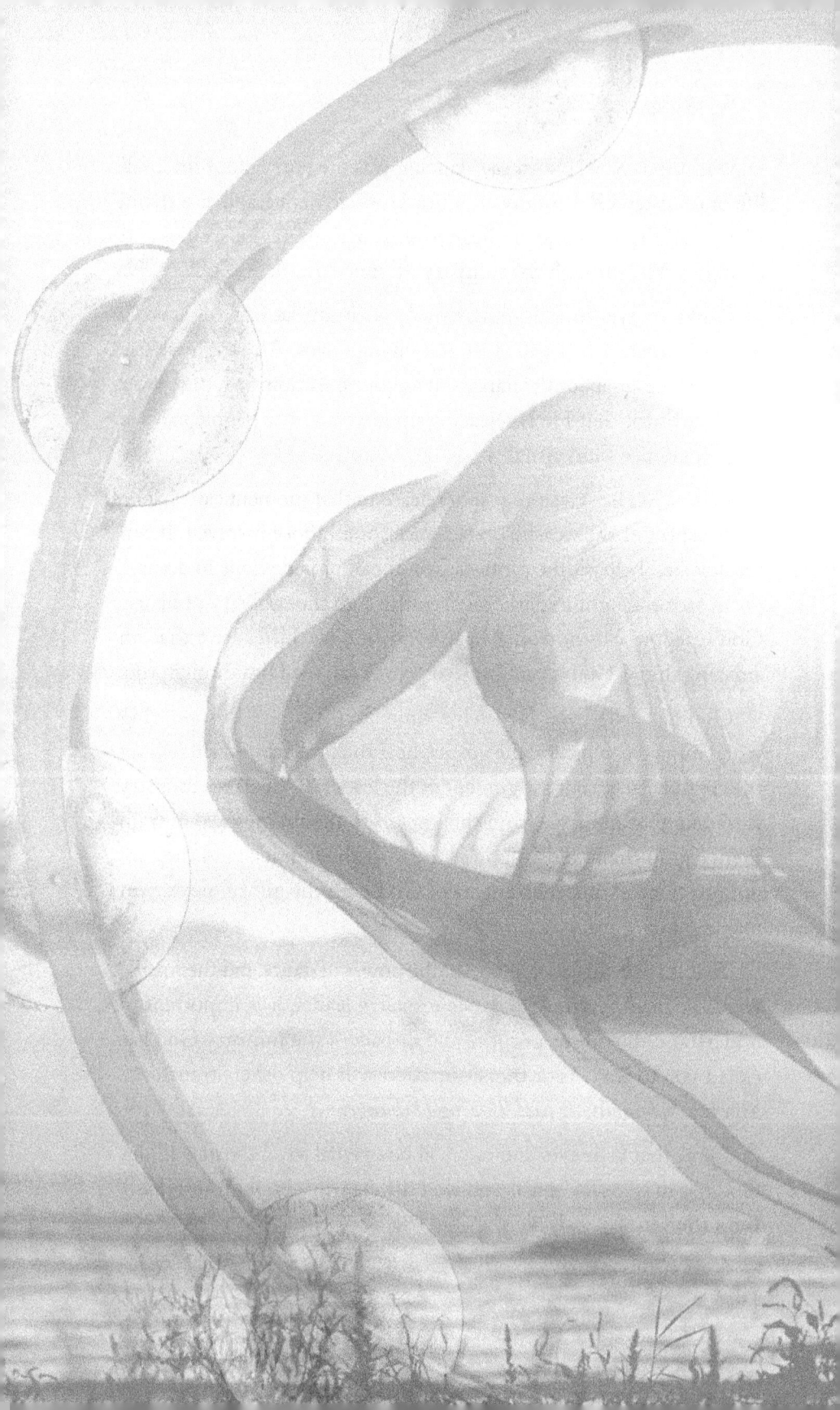

CHAPTER 1

Miriam's Mantle

"Then Miriam the prophet, Aaron's sister, took a timbrel in her hand, and all the women followed her, with timbrels and dancing." (Exodus 15:20 NIV)

Being called as a dance ministry leader

Miriam led the nation of Israel with purpose when she led them in a dance of freedom in Exodus 15:20. The nation was NOW free, and Miriam responded to God in the NOW by leading God's people. Miriam was a prophet as identified in the Word of God; she also was the sister of Moses and an important leader who was instrumental in helping Moses deliver God's people as the prophet Micah released these words from God: *"I brought you up out of Egypt and redeemed you from the land of slavery. I sent Moses to lead you, also Aaron and Miriam"* (Micah 6:4 NIV).

Miriam was more than a dance leader. Not only did she move in the Spirit to release a NOW word of victory, joy, hope and celebration, she got the nation to participate with her. Because of God, things had shifted for the nation, and it was Miriam's assignment to ensure that everybody knew. One of the ways she was able to accomplish this task was leading the women in dance.

Miriam's Mantle is an understanding of who we are as dance ministry leaders. We are more than dancers – we have a role in shifting the atmosphere of worship by hearing, responding to and releasing God's word to God's people, and one of the important ways we are able to do this is through our dance.

When we release God's word, we can change the sound of worship. Miriam teaches us the importance of responding to what God is doing and saying in the now and then releasing it for the people to see.

As we develop as leaders and ministers who can move and respond prophetically (that is, in the NOW word of God), we will change the perception of dance ministry in the church. Folks will begin to see and understand that we are not just dancers, we are not entertainers, we are not to be used just to fill in the program. We are ministers of the gospel who release God's word through our movements. We are the sight of God. This is our mandate. This is Miriam's Mantle.

We are anointed, appointed and called, and therefore we must be equipped and trained, and we must know our purpose, our impact and what we have been sent to do. Let's make sure we understand Miriam's Mantle and do our God-given work.

Do you know where dance is mentioned in the Bible? As part of our mantle as dance ministry leaders, we should know every scripture about dance in the Bible: who was dancing, why they danced and what happened when they danced. *"Then Miriam the prophet, Aaron's sister, took a timbrel in her hand, and all the women followed her, with timbrels and dancing"* (Exodus 15:20 NIV). This is an important scripture because it is the first time dance is mentioned in the Bible. Miriam, Moses' sister, led Israel in praise and worship of God for their deliverance out of Egypt. She played an important role in Israel's deliverance.

The calling of a dance ministry leader

Being called is a privilege – it's an acknowledgment that God has specifically placed you in an assignment for a specific reason. You might think that just because someone is appointed or recommended by someone – a gifted dancer, a long-time church member, a deacon or officer of the church – that in some way this qualifies them to lead the dance ministry in the church, but it does not. Sadly, this is the case. I have seen folks appointed to lead this precious ministry who were not anointed nor appointed by God. This can create confusion and discouragement and can add to the already existing challenges we see today within our church dance ministries.

What's important for us to understand is that we must realize that God has a plan for us to fulfill. Oftentimes we are in ministry, serving in positions, and we have not asked God, "Is this where you want me to be?" We must ask God for His approval, His clarity, His revelation for the assignments that we take on in any capacity. This helps us to ensure that we have God's blessings and anointing to carry out the assignment we believe He has given us to fulfill this season.

When folks are not anointed to serve, or they are in a role for the wrong reasons, it becomes evident. How they operate, their spirit, their willingness to serve, their attitude, and their agenda will often create more conflict and confusion and will impact the ministry from being able to move and serve God's people to its fullest capacity.

If we have been called to lead the ministry of dance, we will do whatever we need to fulfill God's assignment on our lives. That means we acknowledge the calling, we consecrate ourselves and we work toward developing the skills we need to match our assignment and to train and empower others. And guess what? God will give us exactly what we need to do the job He has given us.

A Choregeo spirit

Choregeo (Strong's #G5524) means to be a dance or chorus leader, to supply. In ancient Greek theater, to be a Choregeo was an honor. It was a person who was highly respected because everyone knew that the person, Choregeo, would do everything in order to ensure that the show would take place. They would supply whatever resources where needed, even their own, to ensure completion. "The provision of a chorus at public festivals was a costly business for the Athenian public offices, who supplied in abundance."[1] This word was used metaphorically when the New Testament was translated from Greek to English. We find the word Choregeo in the New Testament two times in two different scriptures:

> *"Now he who supplies seed to the sower and bread for food will also supply and increase your store of seed and will enlarge the harvest of your righteousness."* (2 Corinthians 9:10 NIV)

> *"If anyone speaks, they should do so as one who speaks the very words of God. If anyone serves, they should do so with the strength God provides, so that in all things God may be praised through Jesus Christ. To him be the glory and the power for ever and ever. Amen."* (1 Peter 4:11 NIV)

God supplies – He will furnish abundantly and supply everything we need to get the job done if it's the assignment He sent us to do. God supplies to us, and as leaders of dance ministries, we supply with the strength and resources God gives us. This is why our calling is important and deserves a conversation with God. We do not want to ignore this important ingredient in ministry. God, is this where you are sending me to serve?

Let's look at a few examples from the Bible to see how they responded to God's call on their life.

> *"Then I heard the voice of the Lord saying, 'Whom shall I send? And who will go for us?'*
>
> *And I said, 'Here am I. Send me!'"* (Isaiah 6:8 NIV)

After Isaiah had a vision, he clearly heard the voice of the Lord speaking to him. He acknowledged, surrendered and cried out, "Here am I. Send me!" Not only that, but God revealed to Isaiah what his assignment was and to whom, and although it was not an easy assignment, God graced the prophet to get His job done.

We can also look at Mary, the mother of Jesus. In the Gospel of Luke chapter 1, we learn about Mary and her conversation with Gabriel, an angel of the Lord. Mary was startled and did not know what was taking place. The angel went on to tell Mary God's plan and that He was going to use her to give birth to the Messiah. Mary, knowing she had not been with a man, asked, *"How will this be, since I am a virgin?"* The angel answered, *"The Holy Spirit will come on you, and the power of the Most High will overshadow you"* (Luke 1:34-35 NIV). After the angel confirmed that He would be called "the Son of God," Mary's response was *"I am the Lord's servant. May your word to me be fulfilled"* (Luke 1:38 NIV). Mary said yes. She said yes to God to be used by Him to fulfill His plan in the earth. She was an unwed, pregnant teenage girl with no resources, BUT God supplied everything she needed – the strength, the endurance, the wisdom to raise the Messiah.

Will you be the one to say, "Yes, God, here am I, send me"?

There is a major shift when we say yes!

Our reactions to God can and do vary. You may be full of joy and have a profound sense of wholeness when you get to a place in your life where your God-given assignment has been confirmed. You may also experience fear, or you may ignore or deny your calling. I have heard many stories about people running away from their assignment for years. We are miserable when we ignore God and run away from an area in which God ordained for us to be.

I experienced both joy and fear. I was excited to know God called me, and I felt honored to be able to serve Him. I had an overwhelming feeling of urgency – I needed to get to work! If God had called me, I had lots to learn so I could minster in excellence and teach in excellence. When I realized God had called me, it changed everything: my attitude, my focus, my energy. It shifted my life because I was now able to focus on my calling and my assignment. I was a better minister, a better leader, a better servant and a true worshipper because I knew who I was and that God had called me.

My fear came from my insecurities. "I don't think I can do this! I am not as good as! My technique is not perfect! I just don't think I can!" You know how we do! We can talk ourselves right out of God's plan for our lives, but praise be to God, He will not listen. Deep inside of me, I knew this was what I was supposed to do, so I surrendered and said the same words as the prophet Isaiah: "Here am I, Lord, send me."

As dance leaders, we must know that God has called us into this role and, with His confirmation, have the willingness to do what is necessary. That is part of our leadership mantle. Are you ready? The great thing about our role is that we lead others. Miriam was part of the deliverance team. She was not the appointed leader, but she was on the leadership team. As leaders, we have influence and impact people's lives, especially those we lead. Our next chapter will explore important principles that should guide us as Kingdom leaders.

Points to Tambourine

1. Miriam's Mantle is an understanding of who we are as dance ministry leaders. We are more than dancers – we have a role in shifting the atmosphere of worship by hearing, responding to and releasing God's word to God's people.
   a. Miriam's Mantle is more than just one who leads the dance ministry. What are some of the critical elements of this important mantle that resonate with you?
   b. How has your understanding changed about your role after reading this chapter?
2. Being called is a privilege – it's an acknowledgment that God has specifically placed you in an assignment for a specific reason.
   a. Have you consulted with God for confirmation of your calling? If not, what are you waiting for?
3. Are you ready to go? When you surrender to God, He will supply and furnish abundantly, supplying everything you need to get the job done. Just say no to fear and YES to GOD!

Miriam's Mantle is an incredible privilege. Wear it with humility and be ready to turn the world upside down!

CHAPTER 2

Principles of Kingdom Leadership

Leaders are important and necessary in God's Kingdom. If you are reading this, there is a leader in you. You are born and created to make things happen. Created to be different. Created to change the world. Created to impact the lives of others. As a leader, you have influence. You can inspire and create change. You can release feelings of victory and feelings of hope. You help save lives. As a leader, you are in a position of power, but more importantly, as a leader, you must be under the power and authority of Jesus Christ. He is our leader, and this should be evident in all that we do.

Before we discuss leading others, it is important for leaders to begin with self. How one lives determines how one leads. Below are a few questions to meditate on. Remember, this is between you and God, who already knows the answers to these questions.

- How does your lifestyle reflect the life of Jesus?
- How does your lifestyle contribute to the growth and development of others?

- When you open your mouth, do words of encouragement, strength, hope and love flow out, or do you complain, talk about others and speak doubt and fear?
- Do you study and meditate on the Word of God daily?
- Are you open to hearing and receiving criticism and feedback?
- Are you in order at your house of worship?
- Do you willingly submit to your authorities?
- Do you have a lifestyle of prayer and worship in private?
- Do you tithe?

As a leader, one must be able to self-reflect, evaluate and make changes when needed. What you do, what you say, what you don't do and what you don't say all powerfully affect the lives of those who are in your circle of influence. With or without a title, your power, influence and the anointing of God will be evident in all that you do. As you journey on this road of leadership, there are a few principles I want to share with you that will be important for you to remember.

1. Check in with God – always. *"But seek first the kingdom of God and his righteousness, and all these things will be added to you"* (Matthew 6:33 ESV).

    Before you do anything, you must always check in. As leaders, it is important that you consult with God before you move. The enemy likes to get folks to do, say, not do or not say quickly without the consultation of God. One must learn how, in all circumstances, to check in. God will reveal, uncover and release the specific strategies for the specific situation every time when you spend the time to consult with HIM. Your best weapon against the enemy on this journey of leadership is to make sure your connection to God is secure.

2. Remember you are servants who must be willing to serve others. *"And whoever would be first among you must be slave of all. For even*

the Son of Man came not to be served but to serve, and to give his life as a ransom for many" (Mark 10:44-45 ESV).

A good leader understands this important principle. We serve others. We put others first. We sacrifice. We give, oftentimes with no recognition. You must be willing to serve at all times. This becomes your life. It's not that you are a servant when you feel like it – it is who you are. Leaders serve with humility and grace. Serving others is what leadership is all about. The moment that principle is forgotten, it becomes self-serving. We serve God and serve His people, always. The most powerful, God-fearing leaders are humble and graceful yet can speak with power and authority. When they enter a room, you know there is something different about them. You must take on this spirit of servanthood in order to lead.

3. How you live is important. *"Remember your leaders, who spoke the word of God to you. Consider the outcome of their way of life and imitate their faith"* (Hebrews 13:7 NIV).

Often, how a leader lives his or her life is underrated. More and more, what is accepted – particularly in our churches – has moved away from having leaders with high standards. This cannot be ignored. How can one lead others out of the gutter if their own life is in the gutter? How can one free someone if they are not free themselves? It can't happen! This is not to scare you away but to have you take a good godly look at your life to ensure you are acting and living the way God is expecting you to as a leader.

As the work of the Holy Spirit continues to manifest in our lives, we should be changing. As leaders, we are the examples, and others are watching everything that we do. We want to set the example of how one should live. The Apostle Paul said, *"Follow my example, as I follow the example of Christ"* (1 Corinthians 11:1 NIV). His life was an example of Christ. As leaders, our lives should also be examples of Christ. One of the ways we can ensure that our lives reflect this is to exercise spiritual disciplines. Spiritual disciplines are activities we practice daily to help us stay connected and focused on God. Some of them include study, prayer, worship, meditation, fasting, submission and service. A great book to read on spiritual disciplines is *Celebration of Discipline: The Path to Spiritual Growth* by Richard J. Foster.

4. You must be able to submit to authority. The story of Korah can be found in Numbers chapter 16. Korah was a Levitical priest who was already in a leadership position. He rebelled against Moses after Moses was setting order and structure. Korah was not in agreement with what Moses was doing, so he rebelled and got 200 others to rebel with him. His rebellion against Moses, which was against God because God had chosen Moses, cost the lives of Korah, the others who took his side and their families. They paid the ultimate price – death.

We must remember that, as leaders, we must know how to submit to authority. We may not like the decision, but we must respect it. God gave them the blueprint as the leader. When we fail to recognize power and authority and who God has released it to, we fail to understand the importance of God's choosing. Korah was not Moses. He was not released by God to make decisions, lead the people or change a course of action. He wanted God's power and authority that God had released to Moses, but it was not his to have. God gives us specific assignments, and we need to understand what those assignments are. We must submit and be obedient to our leaders.

I was the dance leader of the children's dance ministry, and the Director of Liturgical Arts, to whom I reported, had asked me to make sure that she see the selection in advance before the children ministered. That meant it was my responsibility to make sure it happened. I had no problem with this direction, as she was the leader. One time, I actually forgot, and after the children ministered, she said to me, "Remember, I need to see the selections before the children minister." I quickly said, "I am sorry," and ensured her that this would not happen again. I could have responded differently. I could have had an attitude. I could have taken what she said in a negative way: "Who does she think she is? Why does she need to see everything? She is only trying to control me." But I did not respond that way. I did exactly what I was supposed to do: submit to authority.

When she was ready to step down after serving over 20 years in that position, she recommended me for the assignment. I thank God that for all the years I served under her, she knew my heart and understood that I respected her, her position and her authority. If we lead others, we have to know how to submit to leadership.

5. Study, study and more study! *"Do your best to present yourself to God as one approved, a worker who does not need to be ashamed and who correctly handles the word of truth"* (2 Timothy 2:15 NIV).

As leaders, we must know the Word of God, read the Word of God and study the Word of God. You must also ensure that whatever area God is calling you to, you study and are prepared in that area. For example, if God has called you to lead a dance ministry, then you need to know about the biblical foundations of dance, you need to know how to dance, you need to understand dance in the church and why it is important, you need to learn about choreographing God's messages in order to be able to release them to God's people. Study helps you learn and grow in those areas so you are equipped. You must be willing to study in order to be effective. You can have a title but not be an effective leader because you are not equipped. As leaders, it is important to know your stuff!

6. Know your gifts. 1 Corinthians 12 tells us about spiritual gifts. You need to know what gifts God has endowed you with. Your gifts help you understand how you operate and function in the body – how God can use you to benefit the church and others. Oftentimes, folks do not know their gifts, so they end up trying to operate in places they should not be. When this happens, it can create confusion in the body of Christ. The enemy also does not want you to know your gifts. As long as you do not know, you spend time and energy doing everything else. Take a spiritual gifts assessment test (you can easily find one online). This will help you understand what your gifts are. Once you discover your gifts and how God wants you to use them, you can then begin to do the work to strengthen them. This will position you to be equipped to do the work God has called you to do.

7. Get a mentor. In 1 and 2 Kings, we read about the story of the prophet Elijah and his mentee Elisha. Elijah was a great man of God who performed miracles, anointed kings and released the very words of God to the kings. He also was obedient and listened to God when God told him to mantle Elisha – to throw his cloak on him (1 Kings 19:19). A good, God-given mentor will hear and see some things that we do not. They may hear from God that there is a specific call on our lives that we have not been able to see or quite understand.

Mentors can help guide, train and mold. Mentors play an important role in our lives, and they can help us develop and grow as leaders. A mentor can pour into us, sharpen us and even push us to new heights. It is a relationship that both participants agree to. If we have chosen a mentor and they agree, we will not be mentored sitting in front of the television. We must be willing to go with them and spend time with them. Visit them in their hometown. Experience them in action. Elisha went everywhere his mentor went after he accepted his call. Close to the end of Elijah's life, he asked his young mentee, *"Tell me, what can I do for you before I am taken away from you?"* Elisha replied, *"Let me inherit a double portion of your spirit"* (2 Kings 2:9 NIV). Then Elijah said to him in verse 10, *"If you see me when I am taken from you, it will be yours."* Elisha could not leave his side. He had to be present at all times in order to see what only God could make visible. We may not be able to be at our mentor's side at all times, but we should make every effort to spend time with them so we can learn and grow.

What are you willing to give up in order to see what God wants to make visible to you? This is not about what is convenient for you, it's about being willing to do whatever is necessary to fulfill the tasks that God is giving you. Elisha was not only present when the Lord took Elijah, we read in 2 Kings that Elisha performed twice as many miracles as his mentor. Elisha was present at the right time, with the right person, in the right place. Mentors are important.

You might have more than one mentor, and that is okay. The idea is that a mentor can pour into you and help guide you. Remember to go to God first and ask HIM who it shall be. God will reveal him or her to you. Sometimes mentors will change as the seasons change in our lives. We must be open to what God is doing in the now in order to continue to move towards our destiny.

Kingdom leaders arise!

God has positioned you for such a time as this. He is molding you for your specific assignment. Not only will you shift, but those who come into your presence will shift as well. Take this season to discover your true self. Know your purpose so you can operate with authority. Stay ignited and keep your fire burning. Your passion will be attractive to others. They will see without a doubt that you love doing what you love doing. Have a vision. You can't go anywhere if you don't see it. Dr. Myles Munroe defines leadership this way: "Leadership is the capacity to influence others through inspiration, generated by a passion, motivated by a vision, birthed from a conviction, produced by a purpose."

God is about to do a new thing! I decree this will be a season of discovering the true leader within you. This will be a season of shifting, where you will move out of your comfort zone into God's zone. Get ready for the new mantles and assignments coming your way. There is a Kingdom leader in you.

Points to Tambourine

1. As a leader, one must be able to self-reflect, evaluate, and make changes when needed. What you do, what you say, what you don't do, and what you don't say all powerfully affect the lives of those who are in your circle of influence.
    a. How often do you spend time reflecting on who you are?
    b. Are you open to criticism, or are you offended easily? We should welcome constructive criticism to help us grow as servant leaders.
    c. What does your spiritual life really look like? Prayer, reading the Word, tithing, giving, fasting, etc. Develop your spiritual disciplines. They will help you in all of your affairs.

CHAPTER 3

Your Role as His Kingdom Leader – Taking Care of Yourself

As discussed in the previous chapter, leaders have influence, so it is critical as a Kingdom leader to ensure one's life is a godly life. Leaders need to take care of themselves not only spiritually, but also emotionally. Emotional and spiritual maturity go hand in hand. One can appear spiritually sound in front of God's people, but behind closed doors, they may suffer from emotional strongholds. These strongholds can eventually impact one's ability to lead.

Kingdom leaders must learn how to manage their own emotions and relate to others. True leaders exhibit emotional maturity. Emotional maturity is defined as how well one is able to respond to situations, control emotions and behave in an adult manner when dealing with others.

Proverbs 16:32 (NIV)
"Better a patient person than a warrior, one with self-control than one who takes a city."

Romans 8:6 (NASB)
"For the mind set on the flesh is death, but the mind set on the Spirit is life and peace."

Colossians 3:2 (NASB)
"Set your mind on the things above, not on the things that are on earth."

Proverbs 29:11 (NLV)
"A fool always loses his temper, but a wise man keeps quiet."

Leaders cannot allow their emotions to be in control. I have experienced many leaders who have sabotaged their positions and contaminated their followers because they have let their emotions get the best of them, or they have lots of emotional baggage that has not been removed. Leaders must deal with these strongholds that impact their abilities to respond emotionally in mature ways. Such strongholds include feelings of abandonment, abuse, neglect, low self-esteem, anger, depression, jealousy and unforgiveness. The important message to note is that if these feelings are not dealt with, then these same feelings will certainly deal with you. We may need deliverance from these strongholds, and Holy Spirit is our guide, our spirit of truth, our teacher of all things. When we consult with Him, He will certainly tell us the truth.

Emotional intelligence

Kingdom leaders must also have some level of emotional intelligence (EQ). EQ refers to the ability to perceive, control and evaluate emotions, not only one's own but also the emotions of others.[2] Why is EQ important for Kingdom leaders? Remember what we discussed in the previous chapter? Leaders have influence over others. Leaders are shifting others. Leaders are leading others to their destiny, motivating others, encouraging others. In order to lead effectively, leaders have to have a keen sense of self and others. According to psychologist Daniel Goleman, there are five key elements to emotional intelligence:[3]

1. **Self-awareness.** Self-awareness is composed of two elements:
   - *Emotional awareness:* The ability to recognize your own emotions and their effects on self and others. Paying attention to what's going on with you emotionally is not easy, but for leaders, it is important to do so. Your feelings can also impact those around you.
   - *Self-confidence:* Sureness about your self-worth and capabilities. This is also important because if you are a leader, people will always have something to say about you, both positive and not so positive. You must be confident in who you are and who God has called you to be. Lack of self-confidence will have you spending time comparing yourself to others, loathing in jealousy and stuck in a cycle that will prevent you from reaching your full potential.

2. **Self-regulation/control.** No one has much control over when they experience emotions as a result of life and situations, but one can, however, have some say in how long an emotion will last or whether or not it takes control of one's life. One can use a few techniques to lessen negative emotions such as anger, anxiety or depression. A few of these techniques include prayer, meditation, exercising or taking walks, or thinking about a situation in a more positive light. Self-regulation involves:
   - *Self-control:* Leaders must be able to manage disruptive impulses.

- *Accountability:* Leaders must be able to take responsibility for their own actions.
- *Adaptability:* Leaders must have a spirit of flexibility so they can handle change.
- *Innovation:* Leaders must be open to new ideas.

3. **Motivation.** As leaders, we must be able to motivate ourselves. How can we motivate others if we can't motivate ourselves? Motivating ourselves for any achievement requires clear goals and a positive attitude. We have to replace all negative thoughts with positive thoughts: the "I can't" to the "I can"; the "this is impossible" to "this is possible." The more positively we think, the more we can accomplish. The more positive we are, the more motivation we have. Motivation consists of:
   - *Achievement drive:* This is our constant drive as we strive to improve or to meet a standard of excellence. This keeps us going and moving forward. Without achievement drive, we have no motivation. Without motivation, we have no movement.
   - *Initiative:* Taking the initiative requires taking risk, readying yourself to act on opportunities that come your way. Doors may open, but if you do not take the initiative, you won't be able to step through those open doors. Fear can immobilize you and prevent you from moving forward.
   - *Optimism:* Leaders must be able to be optimistic despite the obstacles and setbacks that will occur. I have often heard the phrase "your setback is a setup for your comeback." Never let your circumstances dictate your life. You have got to take command of your life and your situation. Speak life out of your mouth. Declare victory in spite of the situation.

4. **Empathy.** The ability to recognize how people feel is important as a leader. The more skillful one is at discerning the feelings

behind others' signals, the better one can control the signals they send to other. An empathetic leader excels at:
- *Serving others:* Anticipating, recognizing and meeting the needs of others.
- *Developing others:* As leaders, we are responsible for helping to develop others. When we can sense what others may need to progress and to develop their skills and abilities, we are in a better place to help them.
- *Environmental awareness:* A group's emotional currents, cultural influences, background, power dynamics and relationships are important for leaders to understand. This awareness allows you to function better in your role.

5. **Social skills.** The development of good interpersonal skills is equivalent to solid leadership. In today's always-connected world, everyone has immediate access to technical knowledge. People skills are even more critical today because you must possess a high EQ to better understand, empathize, talk and negotiate with others in this ever-changing global economy.

EQ is something to continue to work on. It is an important tool that is necessary in order to be effective. A few important questions to meditate on are these:

- Are you easy to anger?
- How do you handle conflict?
- Are you offended easily?
- Do you have a tendency to take things personally?
- Are you easily upset?
- Do you have a humble spirit?
- What's your attitude or temperament like?
- Are you easily approachable?

Your answer to these questions will help you get a sense of where you're at emotionally. The good news is that awareness is the first step in moving forward. Let God do God's work, and allow HIM to reveal to you and uncover what you need to do to be the best Kingdom leader you can be.

A few reminders for Kingdom leaders:

- Be secure within yourself, seeking only approval from God and not others.
- Know your purpose – then you can evaluate yourself based on that knowledge.
- Do not measure your success by the accomplishments of others.
- You must be able to work with others and be open to their contributions and opinions without being offended or taking it out of context.
- Always remain humble. Pride will destroy everything.

"For we are God's handiwork, created in Christ Jesus to do good works, which God prepared in advance for us to do" (Ephesians 2:10 NIV). God made you for a special purpose. You are uniquely gifted and anointed to do the assignment that God has for you. Focus on discovering and perfecting the true Kingdom leader God wants you to be. You will not be disappointed by God's handiwork.

Get ready for the opposition

As leaders, we must also be able to stand up against opposition and rejection. In 1 Kings chapters 17-19, we read about the prophet Elijah and the prophets of Baal. Elijah demonstrated many admirable leadership qualities:

- He had faith.

- He was obedient.
- He put his life on the line to prove that Jehovah was the true God.
- He stood alone as a prophet and challenged the hundreds of so-called prophets of Baal.

The prophets of Baal were false prophets. Elijah killed them all, interceded to break a three-year drought and did a few other things expected of a great leader. Queen Jezebel had heard that he killed all her prophets and she decreed the same fate on him. Elijah ran out of the land, and he went and sat under a tree and prayed that God would kill him because he was overcome by fear. Although he portrayed to the people that he was great, he did not do well with persecution and rejection.

Know that persecution and rejection are going to come because of what you are doing, and because of this, you must be spiritually sound. Remember the spiritual disciplines discussed in the previous chapter. They must be a part of your daily life, because the attacks will come.

2 Corinthians 10:4-5 (NIV)
"The weapons we fight with are not the weapons of the world. On the contrary, they have divine power to demolish strongholds. We demolish arguments and every pretension that sets itself up against the knowledge of God, and we take captive every thought to make it obedient to Christ."

Psalm 46:1 (NIV)
"God is our refuge and strength, an ever-present help in trouble."

Proverbs 18:10 (NRSV)
"The name of the Lord is a strong tower; the righteous run into it and are safe."

Nehemiah 8:10 (NIV)

"Do not grieve, for the joy of the Lord is your strength."

Watch YOUR mouth

Ephesians 4:29 (NIV)
"Do not let any unwholesome talk come out of your mouths, but only what is helpful for building others up according to their needs, that it may benefit those who listen."

Proverbs

12:18
"Reckless words pierce like a sword, but the tongue of the wise brings healing."

15:1
"A gentle answer turns away wrath, but a harsh word stirs up anger."

15:30
"A cheerful look brings joy to the heart, and good news gives health to the bones."

17:22
"A cheerful heart is good medicine…"

18:21
"The tongue has the power of life and death…"

Remember to make sure you speak as Kingdom leaders. Remember we are not bound by environmental restrictions; Kingdom leaders seek and embrace the impossible. Speak encouragement, faith and wholeness. As Kingdom leaders, we must talk about ourselves and others the same way God talks about us. Our words must never be negative or doubt what God can do. Leaders should not complain. We must speak hope, victory and love.

Why is this focus on us? Because as Kingdom leaders, what we say, how we handle situations and people, impacts the emotional and spiritual well-being of our ministry and of the people we lead. We MUST model the way. Folks are watching and paying attention. We must always keep God first so that our Lord gets the glory.

1 Peter 4:11 (NIV)
"If anyone speaks, they should do so as one who speaks the very words of God. If anyone serves, they should do so with the strength God provides, so that in all things God may be praised through Jesus Christ. To him be the glory and the power for ever and ever. Amen."

Points to Tambourine

1. Kingdom leaders must learn how to manage their own emotions and relate to others. True leaders exhibit emotional maturity. Emotional maturity is defined as how well one is able to respond to situations, control emotions and behave in an adult manner when dealing with others.
    a. How well do you handle conflict – or does conflict handle you?
    b. What's eating you? Oftentimes our emotional baggage is a result of unresolved issues. We must deal with these issues. Unless we are healed and delivered, these issues that cause us pain will also impact and cause pain in the life of others.
    c. Are you careful with your words? Our words must never be negative or doubt what God can do. Leaders should not complain. We must speak hope, victory and love.

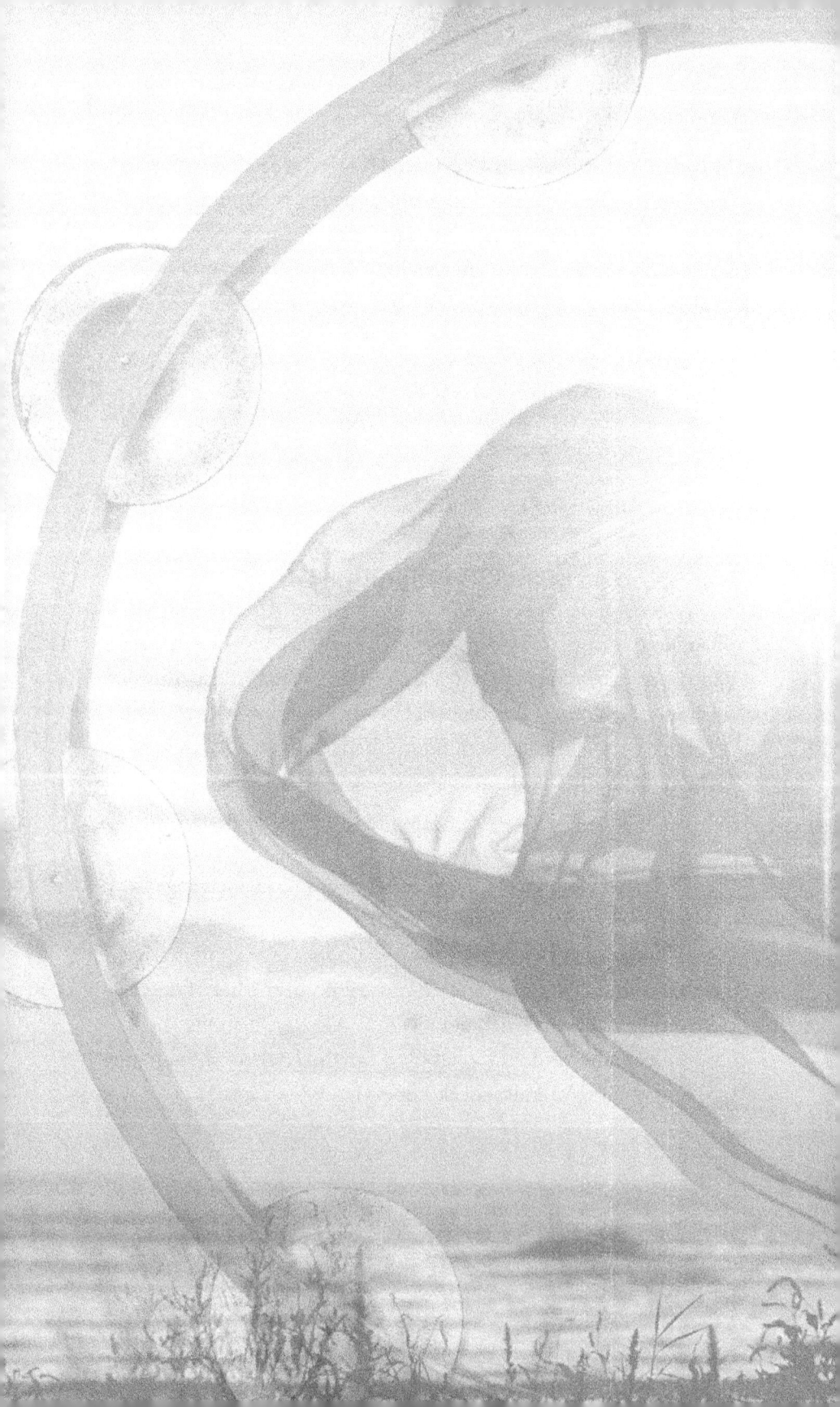

CHAPTER 4

WHAT'S GOING ON?

As the dance ministry leader, you should have a good understanding of the church you serve in and its culture.

Understanding your church is important for many reasons. Before I began to dive into these reasons, let me share some of my personal experience. Our church was in a season of unprecedented change. First, our pastor of 34 years retired. In our denomination, the bishop appoints the pastor. Our next appointed pastor lasted only a few years. His appointment already had challenges because of who he was related to. To top it off, let's just say there was a series of events that were not in good judgment of the pastor. There was division in the church, and the pastor ended up being assigned to another church. His short pastoral appointment left the church broken, bruised, hurt, angry. Many of its long-term members left, and many relationships were damaged. We were assigned a new pastor who had much to deal with as he came into this broken congregation. But I noticed his messages to the congregation. He did not just preach; he preached messages that we needed to hear to begin the process of healing. The messages were prophetic and revelatory, and they also helped us take ownership of our own stuff.

What God revealed to me as the dance leader was that I needed to approach the selections that we ministered to in the same way. It would not have been okay just to dance to a song because I liked the music. God has a specific word through movement that the people needed to see to help them move from where they were into places of healing and deliverance. Now, you may be reading this and asking the question, "Does it really take all of this?" My answer is yes. We must be intentional and be sensitive to our church and its culture, events, situations and dominant spirit. Equipped with this knowledge, Holy Spirit will release what needs to take place. Let's look at some of the foundational things you should know.

Church History. You would think many people would know this, but sometimes folks who attend a church just don't know and don't really care. As the leader, it is important for you to know when the church was founded, by whom, what circumstances surrounded the beginning, etc. The age of the church, who it was founded by, denominational factors – they all definitely have an impact on the culture, the liturgy and who is in leadership.

Foundational beliefs. What does your church believe about God, the Son and Holy Spirit? What about God's word? What about baptism? What about five-fold ministry and spiritual gifts? These and other factors are important and will give you great revelation about your church, and they will be important as you determine, based on the help of Holy Spirit, what songs to minister to.

Leadership and structure. What is the leadership structure at your church? How are leaders and the pastors/bishops assigned? Are they elected or appointed? Is it a family church? Are family members the only ones in leadership? Who is the worship arts leader? Who do you report to, the pastor or worship director? Answering these questions will help you understand how things operate and flow at the church you serve in. It will also help you get things done if you know the proper channels that need to be followed.

Are there any major events or circumstances that have had an impact on the church? As I shared earlier, this is an important area that often can be overlooked. The unexpected or even expected death of a leader or a family member, or a sudden change in leadership, can have a profound impact on the congregation. Understanding what season the church is in is important as the Spirit leads you to minister a selection. Whether it be a song or a scripture reference, all are connected to what God wants to release to His people. When we can get to this place, we move from just dancing to ministering to God's people.

What ministry is valued the most in the church? How is the dance ministry viewed/seen? Nine times out of ten, the music ministry is valued the most in the church. Music plays an important role in ushering in the presence of God, but so does the ministry of dance. In some situations, the dance ministry is valued just as much as the music ministry. In those situations, they work closely together. The point of asking this question is to examine how the ministry is seen, why the ministry is seen this way and what can be done to improve this. Are there characteristics of the music ministry (or other highly valued ministry) that are evident? These are just ways to get the leader to think about moving the ministry in a different direction.

When I took over the dance ministry, we only ministered on special occasions. Christmas, Resurrection Sunday and maybe Women's Day. That's it. I wanted that to change. I believed the dance ministry should be an integral part of the worship experience of the church and that it was important to move from a place of ministering on special occasions to a regular, consistent presence in our weekly services. To begin to make that move, the mindset of the dance ministry members had to shift.

If the dance ministers don't value themselves, then certainly the rest of the congregation will not either. We had work to do. We had to shift our thinking to begin to value our ministry. That meant we had to invest more time and more resources. This took time because folks in the dance ministry were complacent where we were. But to receive the value, respect and appreciation we wanted, we first had to adjust our own perception. Once we broke through that barrier, things began to change for us, and we went from ministering only three times a year to once a month, and then doing praise and worship weekly. We gained new dance ministers, although we also lost dancers because they were not willing to make the shift.

A good practice for the dance leader is to meet with the pastor or designated leader to have a conversation about how the dance ministry is seen. The leader needs to know this from the leadership of the church. If the pastor sees that the dance ministry is never prepared, or he/she has a problem with what the dance ministry wears, the leader needs to know. Often, having these types of meetings generates fruitful results that can shift the perspective and help move the ministry into a new place.

Dance ministry assessment

Now is the time to really take a good, honest look at the dance ministry and the shape it's in. This is not an exercise to feel bad about yourself or the ministry; it is just to help you understand what you are starting with or reshaping so you can develop a plan for where you want to go.

Some of the questions to consider are: How old is the ministry? What do you all wear for garments? How often do you minister? What do your rehearsals look like, and how are they structured? How do you handle conflict if it happens? Are there any guidelines or structures in place for the ministry to follow?

These are a few questions to consider. I have included a copy of a ministry assessment at the end of this chapter. Please use and edit as you see fit. The goal is to position you to develop a plan of action for where you want to see the ministry grow to, and it can help you develop concrete steps to take along with the resources needed to get to where you want to go.

God has placed you in this leadership role to impact the worship experience in your church and to release His word through sight. Not to entertain, perform or as a fill-in, but a revelational, prophetic word for God's people today.

Ministry Assessment

"Keep a close watch on yourself and on the teaching. Persist in this, for by so doing you will save both yourself and your hearers." (1 Timothy 4:16 ESV)

"Intelligent people are always open to new ideas. In fact, they look for them." (Proverbs 18:15 NLT)

"For which one of you, when he wants to build a tower, does not first sit down and calculate the cost, to see if he has enough to complete it?" (Luke 14:28 NASB)

PART I
KNOW YOUR CHURCH!

1. Name and pastor(s) of your church
2. How old is your church?
3. What denomination (if any)?
4. What does your church believe, or what is the foundation of their truth?
5. Is the current pastor the founder of the church? If not, is he/she related to the founder?
6. Has your church leadership changed in the last 3-5 years? New pastor, deacons, etc. If so, please describe.
7. How many members/disciples are there at your church?
8. What is the leadership structure at your church?
9. Who do you submit to?
10. Are you in order at your church?
11. What is your church vision?
12. How many services happen during the week?
13. What is the (estimated) average age of your congregation?
14. What are the top priorities for the church in this season/year?
15. Has there been anything in recent months/years that the church is recovering from?
16. What ministries in your church are valued the most?
17. The least?
18. Why do you think this is the case?

19. How does your call fit into the vision of the church?
20. Is there anything else you think would be important to know regarding your church that I did not ask?

PART II
KNOW YOUR MINISTRY!

1. How does the leadership feel about the ministry of dance?
2. What is the history of the dance ministry at your church?
3. If there is currently a dance ministry at your church, when did it begin?
4. If there is not an active dance ministry, what is the launch date?
5. Were you the founding director/leader, or was it someone else?
    a. Have there been other leaders before you?
        i. Is this a stable position, or has leadership changed several times?
6. How many members do you currently have?
    a. What are the dominant learning styles of your members?
    b. How often do you deal with conflict?
        i. Are you successful in managing conflict?
7. Has there been any growth in the ministry's membership?
8. If so, why?
9. If not, why not?
10. When and how often do you rehearse?
11. Break down a rehearsal. In other words, how is it structured? (For example: Bible study, warm-up, technique.)
12. When do you minister?
13. Do you also participate in praise and worship?

14. Who choreographs for the ministry?
    a. Is there a Bible lesson or a scripture discussed before a new selection is taught?
        i. How are your dance ministry members prepared for a selection?
            1. Who does the preparation?
    b. How many dance levels are within your group? (For example: gentle movers, intermediate, advanced.)
15. Does your church setup make choreography a challenge, e.g., poles in the middle of the floor, speakers, other equipment?
16. What is the vision of the dance ministry?
17. When was the last time you met with your team to discuss the vision of the dance ministry?
18. Do you have guidelines/expectations for the ministry? If so, has your pastor (or the leader you submit to) seen and approved the guidelines?
    a. What happens when members miss important rehearsals?
    b. How do you manage rebellion or disrespect?
    c. Have you ever had to sit a member down?
        i. If so, for what reasons?
        ii. How did you go about that process?
19. Does the church or the ministers purchase garments and/or worship tools?
    a. Do your garments reflect that of priestly garments? (Exodus 28)
    b. Are you properly covered?
    c. Do you wear an overlay over your leotards?
    d. Do you wear leggings or palazzo pants under your skirts?
    e. Have the members been informed about proper bras/sports bras and undergarments?

20. Are there guidelines for hair, makeup, nail polish, jewelry, etc.?

21. What is the scripture foundation/reference for your ministry?

22. Does your ministry have a name?

23. Are there any specific strongholds that have kept the ministry from growing in any area?

24. If there were some things you could do differently, what would they be?

25. Do you have to get approval before you render a selection?
    a. Do you need to run the music by someone else?

26. Is there any other information you think would be important to highlight that has not been covered?

PART III
PLAN OF ACTION

Now that you have completed your assessment, you are now ready to write your plan of action – to *"write the vision and make it plain"* (Habakkuk 2:2 NKJV). Your plan of action will cover things you need to put in place, change, add or take away to EFFECTIVELY complete your God-given assignment. Each plan will be unique depending on your review. For example, if you do not meet regularly with your pastor and/or the leader to whom you submit, part of your plan will include setting up meetings with him/her on a regular basis with expected dates. Another example is that if your ministry only renders for special occasions, part of your plan may be to minister on a regular monthly or bi-monthly basis. Also, you may want to add praise and worship as part of the goal. Details are important, so you would want to include dates/months and/or an expected timeline. If your dance ministry needs garments or training, this is all part of your plan. The goal is to help you write it out so you can begin to implement your God-given assignment.

This is an exciting time as you begin to write God's plan for the direction of the ministry. Remember this is a working document that gives you a chance to pray, listen, write. Write, pray, listen.

I pray that as you begin this process, you will be open to the movement of God and the direction He would have you go. I pray that this be a time of refreshing and revival infused with passion and fire to move to new levels and new heights. I pray that as the leader, you will be able to understand more and more how God has uniquely positioned you for this assignment. I prophesy over your life all the NEW things God has in store for you in this season of planning and preparation. Your latter will be greater than your past as God continues to open doors, providing you with the revelation and the wisdom to complete the assignment given to you.

Points to Tambourine

1. As the dance ministry leader, you should have a good understanding of the church you serve in and its culture.
   a. Have you invested in getting to know your church and its history, foundational beliefs, vision of the leader? These should be important for you to know as the leader. It helps you complete your assignment.
   b. Have you met 1:1 with your church leader or the person who oversees the dance ministry?
   c. What are your goals for the ministry in the next 6-18 months? Where are you trying to take the ministry?
   d. What do you need to work on in order to make this happen?

CHAPTER 5

Choreography with Purpose. I Want to SEE God!

I love teaching choreography. I love bringing God's word to the sight of His people. As dance or movement ministers, we have the ability to impact God's people in a unique way. Bringing God's word to life through movement can set the captives free, release prophetic messages to edify, comfort and exhort, break barriers, open doors, tear down strongholds and create a pathway for God to penetrate the hearts and minds of His people. That is what we can do as movement ministers. This is what distinguishes us from those who are just dancing to perform or entertain people. We have a message from God to deliver!

The purpose of dance ministry or any movement ministry is to edify, comfort and exhort. We are to bring God's word to the sight of God's people through our movement. That means that our hearts must be in the right place. Our dance is not for selfish gain, to be seen or to be glorified ourselves. The one who gets the glory is God. Therefore, understanding our calling is important. It helps us stay focused and grounded in our purpose for dancing before God's people in the first place.

> *Our dance is to glorify God, not ourselves.*
> *Every movement, big or small,*
> *including our facial expressions, counts. They all matter!*

What it means to teach with purpose

pur·pose; *noun*
the reason for which something is done or created or for which something exists.

When we understand who we are as dance ministers and what our assignment is, then our movements and the meaning behind each movement change. Not only do we shift our mindset about ministering before God's people, we begin to choreograph from a different place. We begin to *choreograph with purpose.* When I started to choreograph for the ministry, I would listen for songs that I thought would be good to dance to. A missing piece was that I was not attuned to God and what His message would be to His people that He would therefore release to me to choreograph. (I know, that is deep, right?) I was not thinking about a theme or message or other important factors that would help bring God's relevant word to His people.

I must admit, it took a few years before my process began to shift and I was more attuned to hearing God and then creating to see God. Remember, it is not about the dance. It is about releasing God's word through movement. Although we do in fact dance, if we do not choreograph with purpose, then we miss what God wants to release.

How do I teach choreography with purpose?

When we begin to teach a selection, we always want to ask the question: What is the message God wants to deliver? Is it a message of hope, deliverance, healing? It is a warfare selection to ignite fire for the saints to take back what the enemy may have stolen? It is a prayer? Intercession? When we can answer these questions, it helps us as we choose or receive the scripture(s) and the vision for the selection. Sometimes we may get the message, the theme and the purpose before God gives us the song. Other times, we hear the song and God confirms this is the one, and we then begin to combine the message, the theme and the movements with the song.

Another way to make sure we are choreographing and teaching with purpose is to remember every move counts, regardless of how big or small it is. They all matter. Each movement should have power behind it because when it is released, when the dancer moves, it releases something into the atmosphere. For example. If I am teaching a selection and the theme is deliverance, then as I am teaching a movement, instead of saying "Turn to the left and take a step," I would say, "Turn away from your past, whatever has been holding you back, and step into the new things God has in store for you." This way, the minister can grasp a deeper understanding of what she/he is saying through the movement. Purpose-driven choreography helps to increase clarity.

Another important factor in teaching choreography with purpose is to make sure you have one or more foundational scriptures. This scripture should be discussed and shared with the ministry so they understand that this is the foundation of the selection. It is God's Word that will come to the visual eye. For example, if your foundational scripture is Ephesians 6:10 (*"Be strong in the Lord and in His mighty power"*), what does it mean to be strong in the Lord?

How can we bring that scripture to life to be seen by those who will SEE? As the leader, it will be important for you to teach on this subject – a short teaching, but very important and powerful as it will relate to life. We have, we can, we will overcome the attacks of the enemy! How can God's people SEE this even when life has its many challenges? We may talk about the difficulties and show the hardships of life through movements and choreodrama, but the result is that we are victorious because we are strong in the Lord.

As the leader, you will need to meditate on the scripture, memorize the scripture, let it soak in your heart. Visualize how you can release this to God's people so they can SEE Him.

All this preparation before, during and after will shift the ministry, mindset and outcome of every selection. When the dance ministers understand just how important their ministry is, how important every movement is, how important every facial expression is, things should shift, and when they get up before God's people, they will understand that they are on assignment to bring God's word to His people. We must get out of the place where the dancers are just dancing or moving, or the flags are just going back and forth. No, we are NOT. We want to make certain that we understand this. Even with great choreography and technically trained dancers, I have experienced an empty void because God is missing. Yes, technique is important, but God must be the motivating factor, and the desire of the movement minister must be to make God known, and not for others to see how great of a dancer we are (whoooooo weeeeee).

We are ministers of God's word through dance. We are not performers, and we do not entertain. Our primary purpose is to release God's word. Not to please, not to show off our abilities, but to be humble servants doing what God has called us to do. We have the awesome privilege of sharing God's love, hope and healing using our bodies as a living sacrifice. It is never about us, always about

God. We submit to His will, and we ask for Holy Spirit to lead us and guide us so we will always minister in excellence according to His perfect will.

We have the awesome privilege of sharing God's love, hope and healing using our bodies as a living sacrifice.

Choreography 101

Let's discuss some basic choreography elements to help expand your dance vocabulary. Why is this important? Because there are hundreds of ways to express God through movement, but if our dance language is limited, so is our ability to communicate God through our dance. In other words, *as visual ministers, we help people see God.*

A few important reminders:

- The ministry of dance is visual. *We help people see God.*
- Dance is a language that communicates a message, a story, emotions, victories, defeat, etc.
- Choreography is the organization of the language of dance. This is important because just like we structure or organize a sentence or a paragraph for it to make sense, we must understand that choreography needs to be organized and structured in order for it to make sense. Choreography is "the sequence of steps and movements in dance or figure skating, especially in a ballet or other staged dance (www.oxforddictionaries.com).
- Choreography elements expand the vocabulary and impact the tone, message, intensity and emotion of the piece. Elements are aspects that contribute to the building and creation of a dance, including but not limited to preparation, facial expression, levels, garments, passion, confidence, execution

of movements, use of space, eye contact, dynamics, use of worship tools and creativity of movement.
- We are using the song as a way to enhance the message. What is being communicated? What do you want to communicate? If we do not know what we are communicating, certainly no one else will.
- Always be in alignment with your church leader – make sure you have their okay with everything you do.
- Dance enhances and does not create confusion. It can be an effective ministry or an effective mess.
- Ask yourself the following questions: What is the overall purpose of the dance? What is the theme? Why am I creating this? Is it a prayer, worship, warfare, evangelistic? Does it edify the body, comfort or exhort? Does it glorify God?

Choreography quick tool kit

Directions and levels help give the viewers different perspectives.

1. There are *eight to nine levels* in choreography, depending on who you ask. According to Apostle Pamela Hardy, there are nine levels, as follows:
   1. Prostrate (lying face down on the floor)
   2. Low kneel
   3. High kneel
   4. In a deep plié
   5. Standing
   6. Relevé
   7. Leaps/jumps (body in the air)
   8. Positioned on top of a prop
   9. Leaping off of an elevated surface

2. There are *eight directions* you can work. In other words, what direction is your body facing as you minister to the people? The diagram below gives you an example. The numbers in the circle correspond to the identified directions below.

    1. Face forward
    2. Front right corner
    3. Right side
    4. Back right corner
    5. Face back
    6. Back left corner
    7. Left side
    8. Front left corner

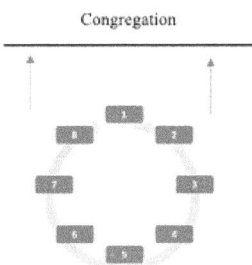

Choreography elements focus on time, energy and spacing. They add to your dance language and give you so much more to do with your movements. Below are just a few basic ones.

- *Accumulation:* Building or adding on. For example: (1, 1+2, 1+2+3) – person 1 starts, then person 2, then person 3 and so on and so on.
- *Augmentation:* Expanding the time of the movement (slowing it down).
- *Canon:* Person 1 starts a phrase/movement, person 2 starts the same thing after person 1, and all people finish the phrase at different times. You can then reverse the canon with the last person who just finished now beginning the canon and starting first. Canons can be done in groups or with individual people (at least two).
- *Connected:* Movement that is connected, meaning someone is always physically touching within the group.
- *Contrast:* Seeing a difference or contrast in movement. For example, contrast can be seen in *levels* (low, middle, high) or in *timing* (half, regular, and double).

- *Curved/indirect:* Curved or rounded, no oppositional angles. Gentler, milder, softer movements.
- *Diminution:* Speeding up the movement.
- *Echo:* Person 1 does a movement phrase and finishes; then person 2 does a movement phrase and finishes. This a copycat effect with no overlapping movement (unlike a canon).
- *Embellishment:* Complementary movement to expand or vary, e.g., turn, jump, gesture or prop.
- *Insertion:* To put new material in the middle of a phrase.
- *Isolation:* Using only one part of the movement; movement of just the arms and/or legs. This is great for different levels, especially if you have gentle movers.
- *Mirroring:* Having a mirror image. For example, one person may be lifting their right arm while another is lifting their left.
- *Oppositional/direct movements:* Opposed at right angles. These movements suggest force or power. Often, we can think of selections/movements that declare power or strength.
- *Prophetic movement:* Spontaneous movement (not planned or choreographed), led by Holy Spirit. *"But the one who prophesies speaks to people for their strengthening, encouraging and comfort."* (1 Corinthians 14:3 NIV)
- *Repetition:* To repeat a movement.
- *Transition:* Movement that helps dancers transition from one phrase to another. Transitions help a dance run smoothly from beginning to middle to end, moving one group in while moving the other out. We can use our aisles, stairs, or front or back of the church for transitions.

These are just a few examples to give you a glimpse of the possibilities. If you are a trained dancer who choreographs, then you are familiar with elements. For those who are not familiar, this will help you see the amazing possibilities that we have as choreographers of God's word. I would encourage you to continue to seek training as a dance leader – ballet, jazz, African dance classes. You will not be disappointed. I would also encourage you to develop further by taking choreography courses, reading books and continuing to expand what you have.

> *"Enlarge the place of your tent, stretch your tent curtains wide, do not hold back; lengthen your cords, strengthen your stakes."* (Isaiah 54:2 NIV)

I prophesy over your life that this is your season for expansion. This is the season that you will come out of your comfort zone and step into a new place in your ministry, in your movements, in your choreography. I speak movement, life, new possibilities, new horizons in your life now. In the name of Jesus and by the power of Holy Spirit!

Points to Tambourine

1. We are to bring God's word to the sight of God's people through our movement. That means that our hearts must be in the right place. Our dance is not for selfish gain, to be seen, nor to glorify ourselves. The one who gets the glory is God. We help people SEE God through our movements; therefore, our movements should have purpose and meaning. There should not be a movement void of purpose.
    a. In what ways do you ensure that the choreography you teach has meaning and purpose?
    b. Do you teach your choreography with purpose?
    c. How do you ensure that dance ministers understand the importance of what they are doing?
    d. Do you always have a scriptural foundation for every selection that is being taught to minister?
    e. Does your choreography include the use of choreography elements? Can you add more?

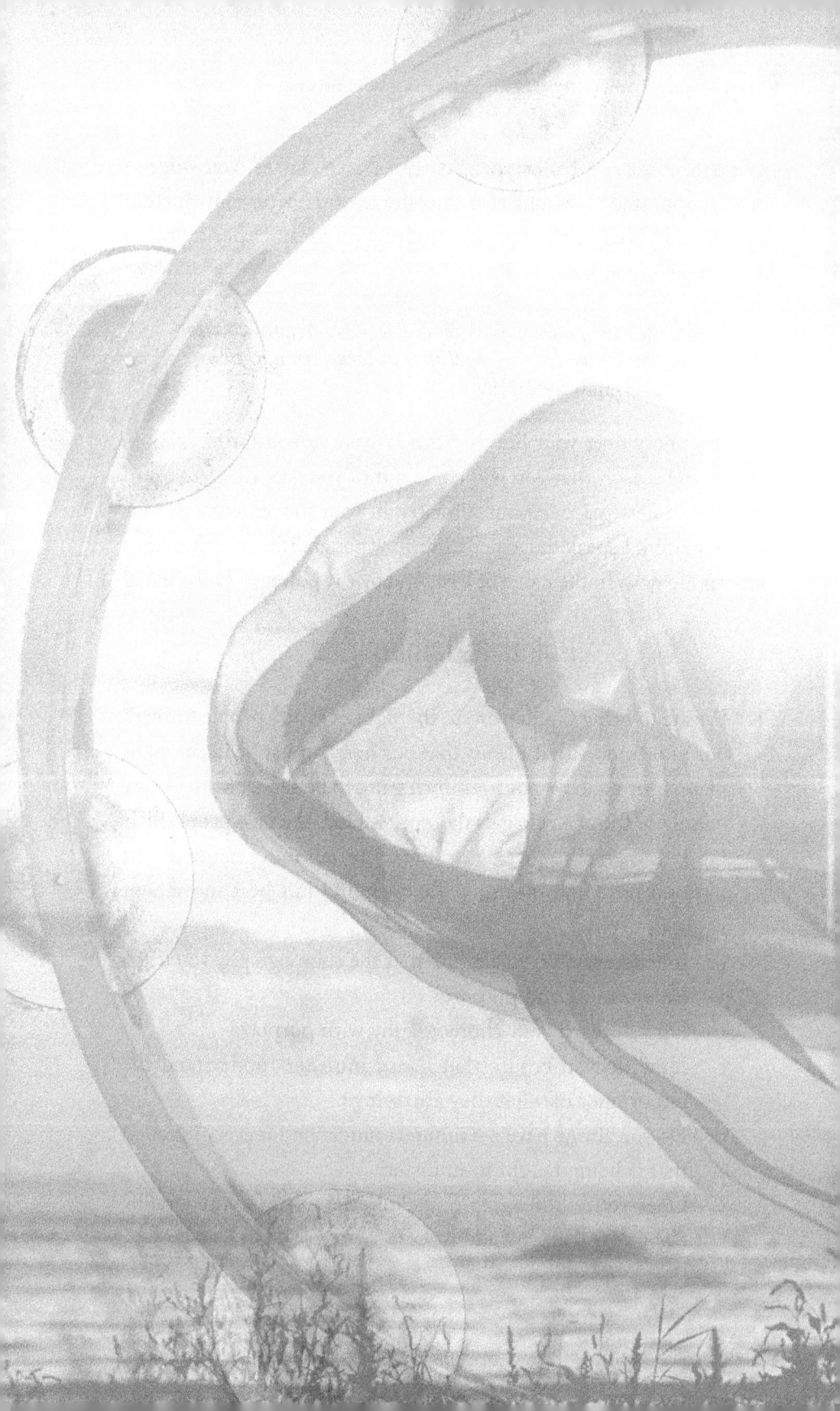

CHAPTER 6

Developing and Maintaining a Spiritually and Emotionally Healthy Dance Ministry

> *"For God is not a God of confusion but of peace…"* (1 Corinthians 14:33 ESV)
>
> *"But all things should be done decently and in order."* (1 Corinthians 14:40 ESV)

What shall we do?

What happens if you live in a household and there are no expectations, no assigned chores, no rules? No understanding of how things should be done or why they should be done? What comes to my mind is CHAOS. We can hope that people will figure it out on their own, but the reality is that if there are no clear guidelines or expectations, people will do what they think is okay. In working with dance ministry leaders over the years, one of the biggest challenges

I have heard many times is that their dancers only seem to show up when they want to or when it's convenient. Another challenge that leaders may struggle with is that the ministry may only minister a few times a year, which means motivation is low and members will only come to rehearsal when it's near the time to minister. Another challenge for leaders is that folks may not understand what ministry truly is – the commitment needed and what it means to serve.

One of the ways to help resolve some of these challenges is to develop and implement some form of order and expectations for the ministry. For a long time, our ministry did not have an order of ministry manual, so for many years, folks did not have any guidelines or expectations. It may sound crazy, but believe me, once I implemented these guidelines, things did change.

The reason guidelines are important is that they communicate important foundational items that sometimes we ASSUME everyone knows. This is a great way to make sure these things are understood by all the ministry members. These items can range from the purpose of the dance ministry and the foundational scripture to expectations for rehearsals and what to do if one is not able to attend. Other topics can include garments (how to care for them, what to wear to rehearsal), expectations for Sunday services, Bible study, etc. These are critical, and yet they are overlooked because the assumption is that everyone knows and understands the importance of each area. Ministry guidelines are a great way to make sure everyone is on the same page.

It is also important to understand that this is not legalistic, religious or controlling. It is a way to clearly articulate the expectations, purpose and goal of the ministry. Folks may resist some of the changes or even have a hard time with some of the expectations, but know that the purpose of this is to help strengthen and build the ministry so that you can minister in excellence. Guidelines help to support the growth and development of the ministry and to move from a mindset of convenience to a mindset of ministry.

Every year, I would review the manual to update the guidelines by adding, deleting and revising the material. This was directly in response to where the ministry was. I would also have a fellowship for the ministry to come together. We would do a potluck, and members would volunteer to bring different food dishes. This was a great way to start the year off by sharing and going over the guidelines. I would also ask the members for their thoughts and feedback as to items they think should be added to or taken off the guidelines.

Finally, I would have each member sign the guidelines to say they are committed to following the expectations. I have seen leaders be creative with what they call this – it could be called a covenant agreement or an agreement of understanding. At any rate, I found that once I implemented these guidelines, confusion and conflict decreased.

Before you implement these guidelines, it is important to have a conversation with your pastor or whoever you report up to in our church. You want to get their approval and make sure they are supporting what you are trying to do. This also helps when you introduce the guidelines, because you can say, "I have met with the pastor, who is in support of these guidelines."

Orientation or not?

I attended Greater Allen Cathedral's biennial worship conference and went to one of the workshops for dance leaders. It was taught by Dr. Kathleen Turner, who is the founding director of the Allen Liturgical Dance Ministry. One of the areas she discussed was the importance of their Genesis training program for anyone who was interested in joining the ministry. The program was six months long and covered all the essentials: what the ministry of dance is, technique, garments, Bible study, etc.

I thought this idea was brilliant, and soon after I came back from that workshop, I implemented an orientation for anyone who was interested in joining the dance ministry. It was a three-month orientation program that covered what the dance ministry is, dance in the Old and New Testaments, expectations, technique and other topics as the Spirit led. I must say it was one of the best things I could have done, because it really gave folks who were joining a solid background and understanding of the dance ministry, expectations, garments, you name it. It was also a way to weed out those who just did not want to invest the time or the resources.

The date and time of the orientation was different from the regular dance rehearsal, and it included only those who expressed interest in joining the ministry. I was able to use other dance ministers to help with the teaching based on their strengths and gifts. The last few sessions of the dance orientation were combined with the regular dance ministry. This was just a way to get them acclimated, to see how the flow was and to introduce them to the team. We made a big deal of the last session because they had invested the time, and now they had made it to the end. We celebrated their completion of the training and prayed with them as they were beginning this new journey.

The orientation, combined with guidelines, shifted the mindset of the members of the ministry. We were never the same. I have included examples of both the guidelines and an orientation outline at the end of this chapter. Enjoy!

Who you are matters!

Who you are as a leader impacts the emotional and spiritual health of the dance ministry you lead. You set the example, you set the culture and you set the expectations. That means your temperament, your attitude and your spiritual wellbeing are major influences in all that you do. As discussed in chapter 2, who you are and how you live your life matters. If you expect a ministry to show up, you must show up. If you expect a ministry to be humble and understand servanthood, you must reflect that.

> *"For where two or three have gathered together in My name, I am there in their midst."* (Matthew 18:20 NASB)

Every rehearsal or dance preparation counts! Review your rehearsals to make sure they are organized and produce what you need. For many years, our rehearsal was very empty and void of purpose. We would come together and quickly dance, and then sometimes we would just talk and really did not accomplish much. What do you want to get out of rehearsal? Why bring folks together if you do not have a plan? Even if you are not preparing to minister a selection, the mindset is that you are always preparing to minister. This means that every rehearsal counts, and rehearsal must be consistent. Rehearsals or dance preparation, whatever you prefer, is the one place where you have all of the folks together and get an opportunity to teach, train, develop, share, inspire. That is quite a bit. Our rehearsals looked like this:

- 6:30 p.m.: Pray in, and then Bible study/reflection.
- 6:45 p.m.: Warmup, which would include some across the floor exercises to help with technique and to build endurance.

- 7:15 p.m.: Teach or review choreography. If we were not learning a new selection, we would review old selections so we would not lose the choreography.
- 8:30 p.m.: Pray out.

Sometimes we would just focus on learning and moving in the prophetic. Sometimes we would just work on interpreting scriptures through movement. Sometimes we would focus on endurance and technique. In other rehearsals, we would practice praise and worship and how to follow by paying attention to the one who is leading, without learning the movement beforehand. We may even do dancing prayers. My point is that every rehearsal would be used to learn and to push the ministers to a new place. This is good to build momentum and to get folks used to coming every week. If your ministry does not minister in church on a regular basis and you are looking to shift, then you will need to make sure rehearsals happen every week.

People want to learn and grow. Our mantle as the leader is to make sure we lead by example, teach, inspire, invest and push. When folks believe they are learning and growing in new places, they will be excited to get to rehearsals.

Teaching/Bible study

As a leader, it is important for you to be able to connect scripture to the selection you are teaching to the ministry. This is critical for a solid spiritual foundation. We must always bring our dancing back to God's Word. I know this may sound elementary, but it can easily be overlooked. It is essential to make Bible study a regular part of your rehearsals, and as the leader, you need to make sure it is included. This can be a part of a movement exercise. For example, you can take Psalm 121, read it together as a group and then assign each scripture to an individual or a small group to interpret in their own movements. Then come back as a group to put the movements together, and then process what that meant – why they chose those movements. This really opens up opportunities to discuss the Word of God and what the scripture means to folks. This can be a great exercise not only to build a team but also to develop the team's dance vocabulary and confidence.

Other times, you may pick a scripture that God places on your heart. This does not have to be long, just 5-10 minutes as a way to center the ministry and rehearsal. You can also have each member take a week where it is their turn to share on a scripture. Maybe it is on a theme, or maybe it is a continuation of the word that was preached on Sunday or the pastor's Bible study, but it should be foundational for the ministry. It helps to ground and center the ministry in preparation for each rehearsal. These are all relevant and important ways to stay spiritually healthy and strong as a ministry.

Sample Order of Ministry Manual

The following manual is an example and can be modified based on the needs of your ministry. The items included in this manual were very specific for our ministry and some of the challenges we were dealing with at the time. For example, one area we had to grow in as a ministry was attendance. Members were inconsistent, and this was an agreed-upon way to begin to hold members accountable. This may not be a challenge for your ministry, but I share these just so you have an idea or something to work with.

An important note: Sometimes you may have individuals in the ministry who may need special attention. This just means that how you respond to them will be unique to their situation. Sometimes they are struggling with commitment, or they have pressing issues on the outside that make it difficult to show up, or they are a gifted dancer but their attitude is off. In any situation, we always want to pray so we are not off-putting but show our concern and love. Sometimes we may need the assistance of a church leader or our pastor for guidance on how best to handle a situation. Sometimes it is the pastor who may need to respond to the person. At any rate, the ministry is a place where we welcome all folks, yet there are specific expectations for how to handle the uncommon situations.

Also, in our church, you are expected to be a member before you can join any ministry. We often get folks who come to the church for the first time, and they see the ministry and want to join. We encourage them to keep coming, to learn about the church and the process of membership. We invite them to come and see how our rehearsals are, and we will walk with them through the entire process to becoming a member.

....

1 Corinthians 7:20	*Let each one remain in the same calling in which he was called.*
Romans 8:28	*And we know that all things work together for good to those who love God, to those who are called according to His purpose.*
Psalm 150:4	*Praise Him with the timbrel and dance; Praise Him with stringed instruments and flutes!*

Mission Statement

The purpose of the Praise and Worship Dance Ministry is to worship God in spirit and in truth and to exalt His holy name. We offer our bodies (temples of the Holy Spirit) as living sacrifices to Him to be used by Him to minister His word through dance. We praise Him and we thank Him.

Joy + Dance x Love of Jesus = Praise and Worship.[4]

Anointing

Psalm 149:3   *Let them praise His name with the dance; Let them sing praises to Him with the timbrel and harp.*

What is the Ministry of Dance?

The ministry of dance is a ministry that releases God's word through movement. In other words, we help people SEE God through our movements using our bodies and other visual items such as flags and banners/billows. Preachers use their voice to help people HEAR God's word; we use our movements and other visual aids to help people SEE God's word. The ministry of dance should always edify, comfort and exhort. It is never about us, always about God's word and His people!

Who Can Join the Liturgical Dance Ministry

- Adults of all ages (male and female).
- Members of the church who have completed the dance orientation series.
- Those who have been called to worship unto the Lord in dance.

Expectations and Responsibilities

Each member of the dance ministry is accountable for the following:

- Attendance at weekly rehearsals, special workshops and technique classes.

- Attendance at Bible study, church school or reading through the Bible.
- Attendance at weekly services.
- Communication with ministry leadership regarding any absences, lateness and leaves of absence.
- Participation in Sunday praise and worship and staying for the entire service.
- Participation in ministry outreach assignments.
- Purchasing and caring for your ministry garments.
- Following and adhering to the dance ministry calendar (all dates must go in your personal calendar).
- Showing respect for all appointed leadership as well as fellow members.

Lateness and Attendance

- It is expected that every member will attend rehearsals on a regular weekly basis, in addition to any extra rehearsals that may be scheduled.
- If you expect to arrive more than ½ hour late, you must inform the leadership in advance of the rehearsal, or you may be asked to sit down and not participate in the rehearsal process.
- If you know that you will be late on a consistent basis, please be sure that leadership is informed of the reason for the consistent tardiness. Likewise, if you need to be dismissed from a rehearsal early, you must inform leadership prior to leaving the rehearsal.
- It is our desire to start every rehearsal on time. With that, all arrivals after 30 minutes of the beginning of class will be considered late.
- If, due to absences or consistent tardiness, you have not learned a dance that will be ministered directly from the

choreographer, you will not be allowed to participate in that dance. We suggest that you continue to learn the dance for the next time it will be ministered.
- No member will be allowed to place himself or herself in any dance without the permission of the choreographer.
- In case of inclement weather, please call _____ to confirm if the church will be closed.
- The leadership of each ministry will email/text members to notify of any rehearsal cancelations or any changes to the schedule.
- The dance ministry is voluntary; however, no one is allowed to choose what he or she will and will not do within the dance ministry based upon desire. After having a discussion with the directors, we will honor your need to sit out of an assignment. Your lack of participation in ministry events and lack of communication will lead to a re-examination of ministry membership.

Leaves of Absence

Taking a leave of absence:
- If you miss *six consecutive classes, you will be asked to take a leave of absence from the dance ministry*. We ask that you please submit in writing a letter to your Director expressing your need to take a leave of absence. Terms for your leave must be discussed with your Director. During your leave, you are still required to attend all special workshops, etc., to remain in step with the current ministry protocols.

Returning from a leave of absence:
- If you have taken a leave of absence and wish to return to active ministry participation, you must first meet with

leadership to discuss the conditions upon which you will be allowed to return. At this time, the Director will share information about what you have missed while you were on leave, including ministry growth, leadership changes, any new procedures for the ministry, etc. Additionally, they will gather information on why you took a leave of absence and understand why you are returning at such time.

- You may be asked to complete any missed reading or writing assignments, and you may not be able to participate fully right away until certain other conditions are met (e.g., attendance at rehearsals).
- Leave of absences for longer than a year may require you to repeat the orientation classes so that you can benefit from the intense teachings and technique classes offered in those sessions.

Praise and Worship

- Praise and worship is an important part of our services. Each member is expected to participate in praise and worship at least 2x/month for Sunday services and other assigned services, e.g., revivals or concerts.
- For praise and worship, you must be dressed and on the floor 15 minutes before service begins.

Materials

- Please bring your Bible, notebook, pen or pencil, personal calendars, water and appropriate clothing every week.
- Please also be prepared to purchase books at the request of the Chaplain or Director.

Rehearsal Attire

Please do not wear any attire to rehearsal that you minister in, including shoes.

- Please wear loose-fitting sweatpants, palazzo pants, or exercise pants.
- Please wear a long (hip or thigh length) and loose-fitting t-shirt or "hankies" (sold by Diane Ransom). Please wear a leotard, fitted shirt, proper undergarments, or an additional t-shirt for additional support and to fully cover your temple.
- Please wear ballet or jazz shoes or be prepared to dance barefoot.
- Please do not wear any jewelry except for wedding or engagement rings and post earrings. It is preferred that all excess jewelry be left at home. We will not be responsible for any lost or stolen jewelry.

Assignments

Dance ministers are expected to read and study all scriptures related to the choreography and/or specific seasons that are given to you in preparation for our ministry assignments.

Additionally, you **MUST** practice what you learn at home as well as listen to the music.

Medical Updates

- Please notify leadership in writing of any medical issues.

Announcements

- Leadership will rely only on email to communicate to the dance ministry. Please notify leadership of any changes to your email address.

Garments

Every dance minister is required to purchase the following:

- *Dance basics*
    - Neutral-colored jazz shoes
    - White long-sleeve leotard*
    - White leggings
    - Blue long-sleeve leotard*
    - Blue leggings
    - White palazzo pants

*** Please order your leotard 2 sizes up as they run small. This will ensure that your leotard completely covers your chest area.**

- *Ministry Garments*
    - White double hankie with gold trim garment (to be ordered from _____)
    - Blue ephod and matching blue palazzo pants (to be ordered from _____)
- New garments will more than likely be purchased once a year. You will be given ample notice regarding the price and style of the garment.
- You MUST purchase a long garment bag.

Garments listed above are for adults only.

Reminders

- Attend weekly services at St. Paul A.M.E. Church.
- Pay tithes and offerings to St. Paul A.M.E. Church.
- Do purchase and obtain the required ministry garments.
- Do make sure that your ministry garments are appropriately cared for.

- Do NOT wear the garment in which you will be ministering to and from the church.
- All rehearsals are mandatory when preparing to minister for a specific assignment. You MUST be at the last rehearsal before we minister.
- Your ability to minister for any selection will be at the discretion of the leadership team.
- Please wear your hair pulled back if possible.
- Clean up all trash in rehearsal spaces.
- Please keep leadership informed of any medical issues or health conditions that you may have.
- Attend technique classes outside of St. Paul and conferences/workshops in order to continue to develop your level of skill as you strive to minister in excellence at all times (dance classes, fitness classes, etc.).
- Do continue to seek spiritual growth by participating in other Bible studies, classes, retreats, etc.

Sample Dance Ministry Orientation

Praise and Worship Adult Dance Ministry

Orientation Series for New Members

"Let them praise his name in the dance: let them sing praises unto him with the timbrel and harp." (Psalm 149:3 KJV)

"And I thank Christ Jesus our Lord, who hath enabled me, for that he counted me faithful, putting me into the ministry." (1 Timothy 1:12 KJV)

Adult Dance Ministry Leadership and Officers

(List names here)

_____

_____

Elected Officers:

(List names here)

_____

_____

Introduction

Welcome to the Adult Praise and Worship Dance Ministry. This orientation serves as a foundation to introduce you to the *MINISTRY* of dance through Bible studies and dance training. During your orientation, you will understand the importance of dance ministry and the associated responsibilities.

Dance Ministry Mission Statement

> *The purpose of the Praise and Worship Dance Ministry is to worship God in spirit and in truth and to exalt HIS holy name. We offer our bodies (temples of the Holy Spirit) as living sacrifices to Him to be used by Him to minister His word though dance. We praise him and we thank Him.*
>
> *Joy + Dance x Love of Jesus = Praise and Worship*
>
> *Anointing*
>
> *12/14/99 – St. Paul Praise and Worship Dance Ministry*

Who Can Join

- Adults of all ages (both male and female).
- Members of the church (if folks were not members, we would work with them to complete this process)
- Those who are willing and ready to serve God
- Those who have accepted Jesus Christ as their personal Savior.
- Those who are Gentle movers.

Orientation Series

The orientation series for new members will consist of 12 sessions. Classes will meet on Tuesdays beginning _____ through_____. All classes are 6:30-8:00 p.m. and will be held in the _____. If there are any changes or cancelations, you will be notified by email.

The schedule for the New Members Orientation is as follows:

(Sample schedule)

Date	Topic	Teacher(s)
9/13	Welcome / Introduction to dance ministry	
9/20	Dance in New Testament/Technique	
9/27	Dance in Old Testament / Technique	
10/4	Are you called? / Technique	
10/11	Foundations – Responsibility	
10/18	Foundations – Attitude	
10/25	The Dancing Preacher	
11/1	Choreography / Technique	
11/8	Dancing Prayers	
11/15	Dancing / Technique	
11/22	Homework assignment, no class	
11/29	Final Assessment	

Please note that in addition to the ministry leader, you can bring in someone to help teach or have others you feel are able to teach in a specific area. (Remember, this is what Holy Spirit spoke to me about in terms of specific needs and areas of teaching. Holy Spirit may reveal different needs for the ministry in which you lead.)

Expectations

Attendance

Attendance will be taken at each session. It is expected that you will attend all sessions, but you will be allowed to miss a maximum of three classes. Any more unexcused absences will result in dismissal from the orientation series. You can join again at the beginning of the next New Members Orientation.

Late arrivals and early dismissals are a distraction. Please plan to arrive at least 15 minutes early. If you need to leave early, please let the instructor know before the start of class. Excessive late arrivals or early dismissals are not acceptable and will be evaluated to determine if you should remain in the session or wait until the next session begins.

Materials

(Here I would add any books that I wanted folks to read.)

Please bring a pen, notebook, your Bibles and a concordance to every class. You will receive handouts at every class and will need them for reference throughout orientation.

Homework Assignments

All homework assignments given by the instructors must be completed and turned in on time. No late assignments will be accepted. If you miss any assignments, you will be dismissed from the orientation series.

Attire

Loose-fitting sweatpants and oversized t-shirts (hip length) must be worn to each session. Females must wear a leotard and/or proper undergarments for additional support. Males must wear two oversized t-shirts for additional support.

All hair must be pulled back and/or pinned down as much as possible.

Please do not wear any jewelry except for wedding or engagement rings and post earrings. It is preferred that all excess jewelry be left at home. We will not be responsible for any lost or stolen jewelry.

I pray that Holy Spirit will give you increased revelation as you determine the direction in which you need to move in terms of an orientation program and expectations for your ministry. I pray that you will have the courage to move forward. I pray that you will get the exact blueprint that your ministry needs in this season. I prophesy over your life that you will be able to overcome every obstacle that is put before you, and that you will move with courage, love and a sound mind. I speak clarity, insight and revelation into your life, in the name of Jesus and by the power of Holy Spirit.

Points to Tambourine

1. The reason guidelines are important is that they communicate important foundations and expectations that sometimes we ASSUME everyone knows. This is a great way to make sure they are understood by all the ministry members. Where there is no order, there is confusion, and where there is no vision, the people will perish.
    a. Are ministry members clear about their expectations as team members?
    b. Do your members know about garments and how to care for them?
    c. What about undergarments, including the right type of support to wear underneath their garments?
    d. Are prayer and Bible study a regular part of your rehearsals?
    e. Do you encourage training?
    f. Have you shared with the ministry what you are trying to accomplish?

CHAPTER 7

BE FRUITFUL AND MULTIPLY

Raising up others

> *"True leaders don't invest in buildings. Jesus never built a building. They invest in people.*
>
> *Why? Because success without a successor is failure. So your legacy should not be in buildings, programs, or projects; your legacy must be in people."* Myles Munroe

Myles Munroe was an incredible leader. His books and his messages have inspired millions of people around the world including me. What was so compelling about Dr. Munroe was his passion to develop other leaders – to train others and to invest in people.

Raising up others and investing in them is so vital. As leaders, we are in a position that impacts other people's lives. When we only focus on ourselves, our own desires and needs, and fail to recognize, train and give other people opportunities, we fall into what I'm calling "pure selfishness." Why would we feel as though we must do it all? We have got to break free from this spirit and begin to give others whom we lead opportunities to grow and to share their gifts. Often, I have found leaders who have struggled with self-esteem issues. Their low self-esteem or their fear of someone else getting the credit takes over, and therefore they respond in a way that is not healthy for the ministry or for that person.

A leader who is able to allow those under his/her leadership to flow in their gifts, help them develop their gifts and allow them to take the credit will develop a healthy harvest. I have often heard leaders say, "I can only do what I am able to do because of those who work *with* me. Not *under* me." Yes, success, or the ability to grow a good healthy harvest, requires teamwork, and a leader who recognizes this will surely develop a fruitful harvest.

What does this look like in action? So glad you asked that question. As a dance leader, I had others on the team who had the gift and the ability to choreograph. It was my responsibility as the leader to encourage them and create the space so they could flow and operate in their gifts. That meant I could step back and let them choreograph. If my desire as their leader is to let them grow and to encourage and inspire them, then this is what I should do.

Low self-esteem and/or jealousy can keep leaders from allowing others to choreograph. Somehow, the leader thinks that this takes away from their leadership. That is so far from the truth, but if we are not spiritually mature, this is an area that creates conflict within the team, because others see gifting, and they see the leader respond in a way that discourages rather than encourages.

We must seek guidance and get delivered from the spirits that prevent us from allowing others to shine. It is never about us. The same principle applies for teaching Bible study or the scripture related to the selection the team is learning. If we are to produce good fruit, we must create opportunities for the seeds to grow. We must fertilize and water their soil with love, encouragement, investments, opportunities and examples.

> *"But the fruit of the Spirit is love, joy, peace, forbearance, kindness, goodness, faithfulness, gentleness and self-control."* (Galatians 5:22-23 NIV)

Our leadership is not to control others

Our atmosphere, or the atmosphere we create for those we are leading, can be very detrimental if it is a controlling atmosphere. There are a few ways that folks will respond if they are in a toxic environment. A toxic environment is one in which the leader is trying to control their members or is leading by authoritarian power. This type of leadership is oppressive, and when those we lead are feeling oppressed, there are a few ways in which they will respond, such as:

- *Resistance:* The natural response is to push back. This type of leadership can lead to resentment, angry confrontations and emotional outbursts.
- *Resignation:* Most of us don't like this type of relationship. With constant conflict, we will leave to look for more promising environments, or even leave church altogether. This leads to lots of church hurt and abuse.
- *Submission (succumbing to pressure):* Submissive followers make little or no effort to think or contribute to the organization.[5]

Our foundation is always to serve, not to control. Servant leadership is the epitome of who we should be and how we should live. Our example not only inspires, it encourages and produces good fruit who have a good example to follow. Jesus is our model for servant leadership, and He teaches, through His actions, what true leadership is.

"Jesus knew that the Father had put all things under his power, and that he had come from God and was returning to God; so he got up from the meal, took off his outer clothing, and wrapped a towel around his waist. After that, he poured water into a basin and began to wash his disciples' feet, drying them with the towel that was wrapped around him." (John 13:3-5 NIV)

Jesus knew who he was and the power He had, and He understood His role. With that, this scripture reminds us that even with power, humility is of the essence. Our ability to be humble in the presence of God and others is a powerful lesson to all.

Jesus trained and equipped His disciples. His example was His life and how He lived. We must always be of the mindset that we are training and equipping others. Those we serve are learning from us in several ways, and we must recognize that at some point in time, others whom we invested in can now wear the mantle of leadership because we have planted good seeds and can now see good fruit. As Elijah threw his mantle onto his mentee Elisha (1 Kings 19:19), we too must be ready and willing to release our mantle upon others. Below are a few inspiring quotes from the late Dr. Myles Munroe about mentoring and producing others.

- "The greatest act of leadership is mentoring."
- "If what you learn, achieve, accumulate or accomplish dies with you, then you are a generational failure."
- "Mentoring is the manifestation of the highest level of personal maturity, security and self-confidence."
- "An insecure person will never train people, they will oppress people."

The importance of mentors

"As iron sharpens iron, so one person sharpens another." (Proverbs 27:17 NIV)

I cannot stress enough the importance of having good mentors. Mentors are people who invest their time, talents and treasures into you. They share with you what God has given them. They are interested in your development as a person, with a desire to see great outcomes for you, your life and your ministry.

In our new age of technology, access to people has increased, giving us unlimited access to online learning platforms such as schools, programs, trainings and conferences. But all that glitters is not gold. We must be careful in this overwhelming sea of "I got the answer you have been looking for." Although I am a proponent of virtual learning platforms, we must be able to discern what is God's and what is self. *"Beloved, do not believe every spirit, but test the spirits to see whether they are from God, for many false prophets have gone out into the world"* (1 John 4:1 ESV). I have seen and heard it all. The same applies for those who will mentor you from afar or through online platforms. It can be very fruitful, but sometimes folks are not seeking the Kingdom of God, just your pockets. Do your homework, ask questions and seek God.

There are different levels of mentors and different types of relationships that we can have with a mentor. As I mentioned, because of technology, we are able to be with folks virtually. This gives us the virtual ability to be in their presence, receive their teaching and benefit from the relationship. There are some people we may call mentors, but the relationship is at a distance. We may not really know them and they may not really know us, but we follow them on social platforms, know of their work, read their publications and travel to see and hear them whenever possible. I like to call these types of folks "cloud-based" or "virtual-based mentors." An example for me is Bishop Corletta J. Vaughn. I met her when we she came to a church I served in before I was sent to pastor a church. She was there for the entire weekend. Although I knew of her before she came, this was a great opportunity for me to meet her in person.

After she came, I was able to follow her on Facebook, and then I found out she had a training and mentoring program for women preachers. This was exciting for me because it was a way for me to glean from her on a regular basis, to have access to her teachings and to connect virtually. She has a monthly time for those of us in the group to meet with her, and she is on Facebook daily for "Pentecost in a Pandemic" where she teaches about Holy Spirit.

This has been a blessing for me, especially because she has the experience of being in a denomination as a leader, yet part of her mandate is to free people from religious bondage. She understands the issues and the politics, and she has navigated the waters doing what she has been called to do. Even though it was not and is not easy for her, she is an Apostle of the Lord Jesus Christ, elected, ordained and consecrated as a bishop, overseeing many churches and ministries, and she is a pastor of a Baptist church. Wow. She is a great example for me for many reasons, and I always get incredible insight and revelation because she has been there herself. We do not have a close personal relationship, yet she is one I can say has my ear and I listen.

Another mentor relationship worth mentioning is one that is much more involved. Dr. Pamela Hardy has been an incredible mentor to me for the last several years. Those of you who are reading this book may know of her. She is the Founder/Apostle of the Eagles International Training Institute, an apostolic training network to equip the saints for works of service in the kingdom. I graduated from their Dance Year 1 program in 2009, and my life was totally changed.

It was about five years later that I officially asked her to be my mentor. When we spoke on the phone, she said yes, but added, "You need to come and travel with me." I did not understand why at the time, but now I do. I was able to spend time with her up close. I was able to experience how she operated and how the Spirit of the Lord moved in her and through her. I was able to hear from her and be with her in a way that you don't get virtually. I traveled to many nations with her and grew exponentially in ministry as God continued to open my eyes. Today she is still a very important person in my life. I still learn from her and consider her one of my great leaders. She has been a blessing to me and to many others in the Kingdom of God.

Although there are many other extraordinary women leaders, dance ministers and pastors who have influenced my life tremendously, for the purpose of this book, I wanted to mention these two to give you an example of the different types of mentor relationships that I referenced. These are incredible women who have helped shape my ministry and life. I share these stories to help you understand the significance of mentorship in my life and how much I value insight and information from those whom God has called. They have pushed me and pulled things out of me I did not know were even there, and for that, I am grateful.

A note about Apostle Vaughn and Apostle Pamela. Both women have a heavy apostolic anointing, and if you do not understand the five-fold ministry and the ministry of the Apostle, you may miss what God is doing. Apostles are pioneers; they break up and lay foundations. They are not worried about making you feel good but are concerned about propelling you into your destiny. Some folks can't handle that. I am so glad God sent them my way and that I caught the revelation. My ministry, my life, my teaching and preaching, all led by Holy Spirit, have been blessed by their ministry.

Points to Tambourine

1. A leader who is able to allow those under his/her leadership to flow in their gifts, help them develop their gifts and allow them to take the credit will develop a healthy harvest.
    a. How often do you allow others to use their gifts in the ministry, e.g., choreograph, teach Bible study as it relates to the ministry piece you are learning, lead warmup, lead prayer?
    b. If you have a team, do you always feel as though you have to do everything? If so, why?
    c. Do you encourage, inspire and teach, or do you discourage and criticize?
    d. Are you actively developing leaders for their next?
    e. What type of fruit are you producing?

CHAPTER 8

READY, SET, GO!

Empower
- to give (someone) the authority or power to do something
- to make (someone) stronger and more confident

Often, I would hear these familiar words: "I can't." These words destroy all attempts to even try. It creates the mindset that there is no possibility, no next, no new! "I can't" is a deadly, destructive end that produces no fruit. *"The tongue has the power of life and death…"* (Proverbs 18:21 NIV). As leaders, we are the cheerleading team and the coach. We are the ones who will empower, encourage and strengthen. We will be the ones to say "YES YOU CAN."

This makes all the difference in the world. I think of the many times I choreographed for gentle movers. They would sometimes be full of fear and feel as though they were not as important as the other more advanced dancers, that maybe their movements were not as good or that they were not even really needed. My role in leading them was to shift that perspective, to teach, to encourage and to empower them. I would say, "Yes, you are important! That was great! Yes, you can do this! You look beautiful! That's it, you are doing a great job!" Patiently, I would teach the movement, modify it if necessary and take the time to show them the movement. By the time we finished, they were ready, feeling encouraged and like they belonged. They were empowered to complete their assignment.

We must be the ones to empower folks to act, to do, to go beyond their norm. We must empower them to know that they can push forward, move barriers and beat their Goliath. Sometimes folks will come into the dance ministry already broken, wounded – they may have low self-esteem or rejection issues. Although we cannot resolve those issues, we certainly do not want to reinforce them. Our prophetic voices give life to dead situations. We help people push out of them what they did not realize was inside of them. Our ability to empower the team pushes them to go beyond the norm. It encourages them to do what they may feel they can't do. The body of believers needs to be strengthened, encouraged and comforted. The simplest words, "God has His hands on you," can help someone feel as though it will be all right in the midst of their storm, and guess what? That is the Spirit of Prophecy at work.

Prophecy is part of Miriam's Mantle. She was a prophet, and she not only led the people in dance and worship but also spoke God's words to God's people. We must remember our role is much more than just dancing. We may not sit in the office of a prophet, but we can all operate in the spirit of prophecy. *"But the one who prophesies speaks to people for their strengthening, encouraging and comfort"* (1 Corinthians 14:3 NIV). *"...For it is the Spirit of prophecy who bears testimony to Jesus"* (Revelation 19:10 NIV).

Our ability to empower the team we lead will be reflected as they are ministering before God's people. With the power, strength and encouragement that they have been given, they now will be able to release that same encouragement, strength and power to the people they are ministering to.

Imagine a man or women who is preaching God's word through their mouth, but somehow their belief in what they are saying does not come through in their voice. In fact, we may hear uncertainty or confusion. It is the same with our dance. As leaders, we must help the dance ministers understand their prophetic voice when it comes out through their prophetic movements. In other words, as dance ministers, we are a prophetic voice. We edify, comfort and exhort through our movements. So, the more we understand this as leaders, the more we are able to teach and empower the ministry in this area.

The sending and release

"'…As the Father has sent me, I am sending you.' And with that he breathed on them and said, 'Receive the Holy Spirit.'" (John 20:21-22 NIV)

"All authority in heaven and on earth has been given to me. Therefore go and make disciples of all nations, baptizing them in the name of the Father and of the Son and of the Holy Spirit, and teaching them to obey everything I have commanded you. And surely I am with you always, to the very end of the age." (Matthew 28:18-20 NIV)

There is nothing more empowering and Spirit driven than when we can send and release the saints to do the assignment that God is sending them to do. As dance ministers, our assignment is to release God's word through dance – to communicate His message to His people. Our mantle as dance ministry leaders requires us to send and release our team to GO and do with all power and authority given to us in the name of the resurrected Lord and Savior Jesus Christ and by the power of Holy Spirit to go and fulfill the assignment. Go and minister in dance to God's people. Go and dance with all your heart and all your mind. Go and dance and shift the atmosphere. Go and minister through dance to change people's lives, to set the captives free, to release miracles, healing and deliverance.

Go. Go. Go. Go and do what we believe God has called us to do. When we operate from that place, it changes how we dance. It changes how we think. It even changes how we move as we get into position to begin to minister our dance. Leaders, we must release the sounds of deliverance, the spirit of deliverance, strength and victory in our dancers. We must ensure that they GO with a song of victory in their dance. That means we send them based on what we impart in them. We empower them to do great things by our words. Jesus did not send His disciples to do nothing. He did not send His disciples to chill out on the couch. He sent them to continue His work – to preach, heal, deliver and help set the captives free.

Leaders, we have been given the mantle to preach and prophesy through our dance, to heal, to deliver and help set the captives free. This is Miriam's Mantle. She FEARED GOD, she LED the women and the nation of Israel in DANCE. She PROPHESIED, and she helped SET THE CAPTIVES FREE.

Miriam's Mantle

I pray that as you finish this book, you have begun to understand and appreciate Miriam's Mantle. I pray that you accept the mantle that has been given to you and wear it with humility, with a desire to be a true vessel for God, allowing Him to use you in a mighty way. I pray that this be the beginning of your new next, as you take on the Mantle of Miriam and go to new levels of worship, understanding and revelation.

I prophesy that as you walk and serve wearing Miriam's Mantle, God will continue to open doors, remove barriers and release upon you a grace that will set the captives free. I prophesy that your dancing will never be the same, your choreography will shift, your understanding will shift. I prophesy that the muzzle will come off your mouth and you will begin to prophesy. You will not stay quiet. There will be a new sound that will come from your mouth, and it will penetrate your region, your community, your church.

As you continue in your next season, I know God will reveal to you whom to throw your cloak on. You will train, impart, encourage and release to continue the work of God's Kingdom.

Points to Tambourine

1. We must be the ones to empower folks to act, to do, to go beyond their norm. We must empower them to know that they can push forward, move barriers and beat their Goliath.
    a. Are you empowering your team to go beyond, to move out of their comfort zone in a loving way?
    b. Do you treat all members with respect and help them feel just as important even if they are not trained dancers? (Gentle movers are just as important!)
    c. Do you modify the movements for gentle movers so they can feel good about what they are doing?
    d. Do you pray as a team before you minister, and do you empower and send your team with power and authority to go and do what God is sending them to do?

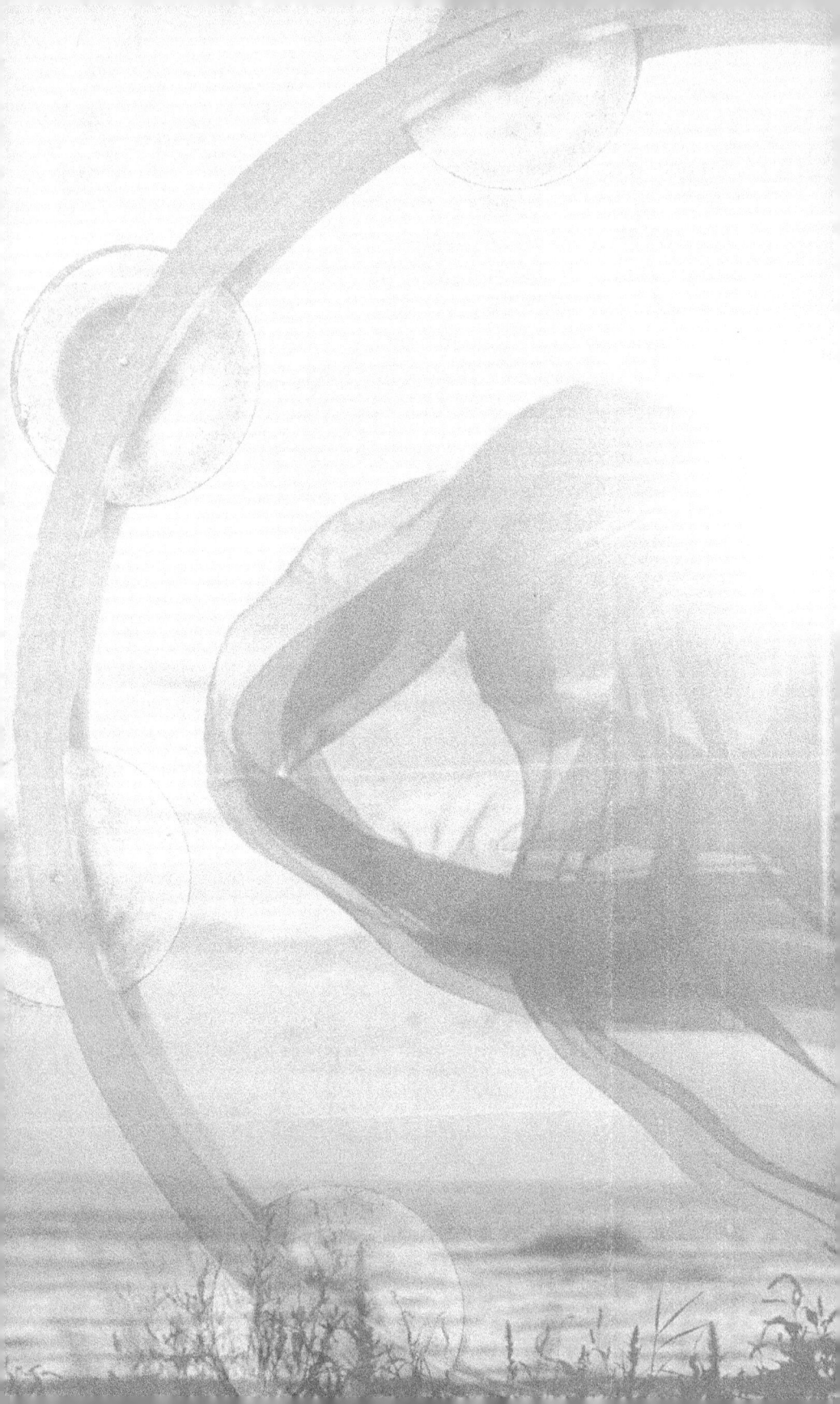

Conclusion

Now that you have read this book, my prayer is that you understand what a difference you make as the dance ministry leader. What a difference a dance ministry leader makes! How we operate, function, teach, share, lead, pray, move, study and grow all impact the ministry that we lead. The ministers we lead become the DNA we impart in them. This is how important our role is and how much of a difference we make. When we embrace our role, we humbly accept, with a servant spirit, Miriam's Mantle.

Many folks are just dancing, not ministering. My goal in this book has been to help you understand not just the difference between dancing and ministering in dance, but also the difference between a leader who is leading just because, and a leader who knows his/her mandate given by God to impact His Kingdom.

I was fortunate to have been trained before I got the mandate to lead. I went through Eagles International Training Institute, as I mentioned earlier, and that prepared me for my next. I already knew I was called to the dance ministry, but when I was elevated to lead the dance ministry and the liturgical arts department, I knew this is what I was sent to do. I was ready to shake up and shift the worship experience of the people. I was ready to transform our dance, our sound, our movements. I was ready to ensure that the dance ministry became an important part of the fabric of our worship experience. I was ready to put in the time, the resources, the studying, whatever it took, because that was my assignment. I was ready to change what needed to be changed, and to hear from others what needed to be changed. I was ready! And now I release that same spirit upon you. A spirit of readiness to go and do what God has called you to do. A spirit of openness to receive all that God has for you, and a spirit of fire to ignite everything around you, to penetrate areas that have not been penetrated before.

Being trained and equipped changed everything for me, and being around other dance leaders who had been around, who understood their mantle, who had the experience as a dance ministry leader was one of the best things I ever could have done for myself and for those I led.

As we grow, the ministry grows. If we stay still, the ministry will stay still, except for those individuals in the ministry who know that there is more for them to learn. God will make certain they get what they need to complete the assignment they have been called to do.

I hope this book encourages you to move to another level in your ministry, and to be excited about this incredible opportunity to impact lives in God's Kingdom. I pray that your eyes have opened even more, and that you have even changed. I pray you will be ignited to get training and to invest resources into yourself and others. I pray you will have the courage to dig deep and seek God for guidance and hear what He says.

I pray that in this coming season, your mantle will move you into a new realm of insight, revelation and wisdom. I pray that your relationship with God will continue to grow, and that your choreography will be a manifestation of your growth and your deeper relationship with God.

"…In him we live, move and have our being…" (Acts 17:28 NIV)

The ministry of dance has come a long way from over 40 years ago when it first started to appear in churches. One of those churches was St. Paul A.M.E. Church in Cambridge, MA. They wanted to bring the word of God to God's people through dance. They wanted people to see God. They had a heart for God and His people, and they loved Him so much that their expression for that love was manifested through their movement. We take our deep love, reverence, worship, repentance, deliverance, hope, freedom, salvation, grace, mercy, forgiveness, kindness, joy, and share all of these and more though our dance. Every part of our being, from the crown of our heads to the soles of our feet. We release into the atmosphere God's message – not ours, not our favorite song, not our favorite movements but God's message.

I prophesy that every turn you make will bring you closer to your destiny, that every leap you take will expand your territory. I prophesy that every time you raise your hand, you will grab hold of God's promises, and for every relevé, you will soar to new heights. Every time you plié, you will receive an overflow of God's abundant joy, and every time you wave your arms back and forth, up and down, there will be a fresh outpouring of Holy Spirit upon your life. Move. Move. Move, and release all that God has in store for you!

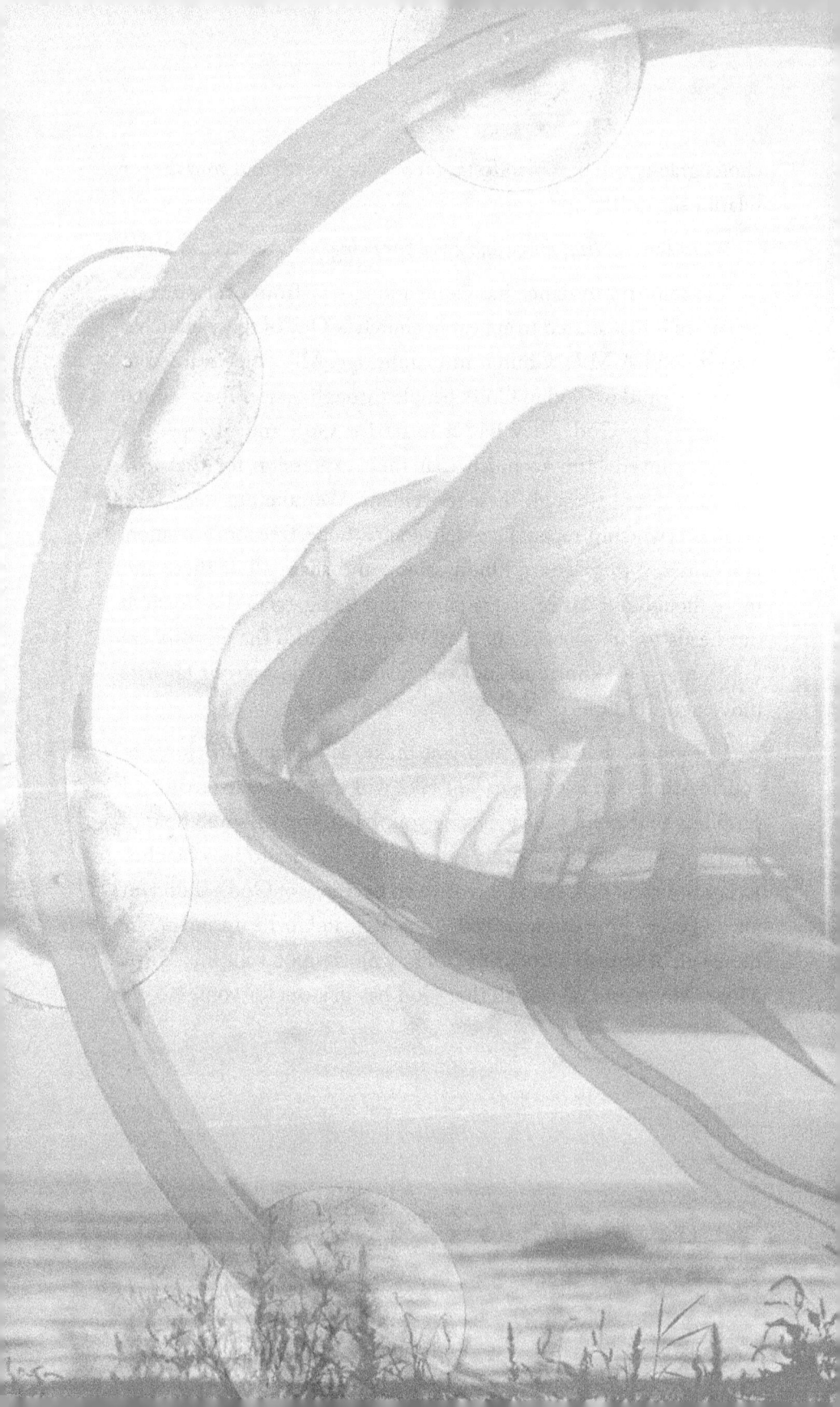

Endnotes

1. BibleApps.com, "5224. chorégeó," https://bibleapps.com/greek/5524.htm

2. Psychology Today, "Emotional Intelligence," https://www.psychologytoday.com/us/basics/emotional-intelligence

3. MindTools, "Emotional Intelligence in Leadership," https://www.mindtools.com/pages/article/newLDR_45.htm

4. This formula was created by members at St. Paul A.M.E. Church, Cambridge, MA 02138.

5. Myles Munroe, Becoming A Leader (New Kensington, PA: Whitaker House, 2009), 110, Kindle.

NOTES

Notes

Notes

Notes